EDUCATOR'S GUIDE TO COLLECTIVE NEGOTIATIONS

Educator's Guide to Collective Negotiations

Thomas P. Gilroy, Program Director
Center for Labor and Management
University of Iowa

Anthony V. Sinicropi, Associate Director
Center for Labor and Management
University of Iowa

Franklin D. Stone, Professor
College of Education
University of Iowa

Theodore R. Urich, Assistant Professor
Department of Education
Purdue University

Charles E. Merrill Publishing Company
Columbus, Ohio   *A Bell & Howell Company*

Merrill's Series for Educational Administration

under the Editorship of

Dr. Luvern L. Cunningham, Dean
College of Education
The Ohio State University

and

Dr. H. Thomas James, Dean
School of Education
Stanford University

Copyright © 1969 by Charles E. Merrill Publishing Company, Columbus, Ohio. All rights reserved. No part of this book may be reproduced, by mimeograph or any other means, without permission in writing from the publisher.

Library of Congress Catalog Card Number: 69-12379

1 2 3 4 5 6 7 8 — 72 71 70 69 68

Printed in the United States of America

Introduction

"Collective negotiations" is a new term popularized by Myron Lieberman and Michael H. Moskow. It is a hybrid term, borrowing from the old, traditional "collective bargaining" and the new but often-used "professional negotiations." It epitomizes the uniqueness of bargaining in the public school field and yet reflects the fact that many of the developments in this area have grown out of the experiences of the past.

The process of collective negotiations has indeed become evident to an extent beyond most of our expectations, particularly since the advent of the 1960's. There is not a single area of the nation—urban or rural, large or small, industrial or agricultural, rich or poor, northern or southern, eastern or western—that has been immune to the developments in teacher bargaining. While the pace has varied, the influence nonetheless has been significant; what is even more important, there is every indication that collective negotiations will continue to develop in the future and have a significant impact upon American education.

Many factors have accounted for the fast rise of collective negotiations. Below are listed a few of those factors which are often referred to as the most significant:

- Executive Order 10988: a directive by the Kennedy Administration in 1962 authorizing collective bargaining for federal employees;
- the passage of several state statutes since 1960 authorizing and/or promoting collective bargaining for state and public employees (including teachers);
- the continued growth of white-collar workers who, since 1955, have exceeded the number of blue-collar workers;
- the growth in public employment (including teachers)—the fastest-growing employment sector of the economy;

- the strong national and local interest in the public school system as evidenced by the expansion of physical facilities to care for the burgeoning increases in students;
- the increasing role of the federal government in the public primary and secondary school systems;
- the emphasis by public unions such as the AFT, AFSCME, and AFGE as well as the NEA and other groups such as the ANA (nurses) to recruit new members;
- the continued economic growth of the nation—(sixty-four months of uninterrupted economic prosperity);
- the general social and civil unrest sweeping the nation.

It is important to note that all of these factors do not uniformly affect each and every community but that each factor does have a local impact, no matter how indirect. When taken into account in combination, the overall effect appears to be exponential.

Collective bargaining in the traditional sense has been maturing for over thirty years in American private industry. While the school situation is indeed different from that of the private sector, there are undoubtedly many benefits which might be realized by the schools in attempting to capitalize on these three decades of experience. There is no need for those in the educational field to waste years in developing rules of bargaining—be they legal, economic, psychological, or social.

When planning this book, the authors had in mind the local school district and the actors who might be involved in a negotiations session for the first time or, perhaps, those with only limited experience. The expert who has gone through a number of bargaining and negotiating experiences will already be familiar with the ideas expressed here.

The book attempts to be nonpartisan to either teachers, administrators, or to the several organizations which represent both groups. It should prove helpful to the local board member, the school superintendent, the principal, the teacher, and the student of education. Both the AFT and NEA organizations are described and the positions generally taken by such organizations are explained.

The volume is a guide outlining some of the background and framework with which collective negotiations are most often associated. This is not a "how to do it" kit since the bargaining phenomenon is a "people" phenomenon; consequently, hard-and-fast

Introduction

procedures are not meaningful and, perhaps, impossible to develop. The book is broken into seven sections:

Chapter 1: an outline of the changing relationships in education;

Chapter 2: a discussion of the organizational and legal structure of collective negotiations;

Chapter 3: an explanation of the procedures and techniques of collective negotiations;

Chapter 4: a brief discussion of the language of collective negotiations in which terms are defined by their most commonly accepted meanings;

Chapter 5: a series of questions typically asked about collective negotiations with answers to these questions;

Chapter 6: a hypothetical case study dealing with the first approach to formal collective negotiations in the school district;

Chapter 7: a selection of services and references of value to people involved in collective negotiations.

Contents

Chapter 1 1

Changing Relationships in Education
    Bureaucratization, 2
    Today's Teachers, 3
    The Role of Behavioral Theory, 4
    Society and the Law, 5
    Conclusion, 6

Chapter 2 9

Organizational and Legal Structure of Collective Negotiations
    The Right to Organize and Bargain Collectively, 10
    Recognition and the Bargaining Unit, 14
    Criteria for Determining an Appropriate Unit, 15
    Types of Representation, 16

Method of Recognition, 17
Duration of Recognition, 19
The Scope of Collective Negotiations, 20
Conclusion, 22

Chapter 3

Procedures and Techniques in Collective Negotiations

What Is Collective Negotiation? 25
Why Collective Negotiations? 26
How to View Collective Negotiations—Some Structures, 27
Negotiations, Ritualism, and the Individual, 28
Preparation for Negotiations, 30
Preparations for Negotiation for Management and the Employee Organization, 30
Who Should Negotiate? 33
Special Note on the Role of Attorneys and Board Members, 34
How Should Negotiation Proceed? 34
Negotiations in Relation to the Teacher Organization, the Board, and the Public, 38
Negotiations in Relation to the Membership for the Teacher Organization, 38
Negotiations: The Administer's Relationship with the Board and his Fellow Administrators, 40
Contract Negotiations in Relation to the Community, 42
What to Negotiate, 42
The Written Agreement, 43
Administering the Agreement, 44

Chapter 4

The Language of Collective Negotiations

Quality in Communications, 47
Words and Phrases Defined, 48

Chapter 5   57

Questions and Answers

    The Teacher Organizes, 57
    Teacher Organizations, 60
    Authority and Will to Negotiate, 62
    The Negotiators, 63
    The Superintendent's Role, 64
    The Administrator and Employee Organizations, 67
    Negotiating Sessions, 68
    Negotiable Items, 70
    Recognition, 72
    Reaching an Impasse, 76
    Grievance Procedures, 79
    Some Other Questions, 80

Chapter 6   83

Hypothetical Case Study: Organization and Collective Negotiations in Public Education

    Organization of Teachers, 85
    Planning for Teacher Recognition, 86
    Preparation for the First Negotiations: The School Board, 89
    Preparation for the First Negotiations: The Teachers, 91
    Getting to the Negotiating Table, 93
    The Negotiation Process, 95
    Dialogue—Second Session: Priority of Demands, 95
    The Sixth Session: Further Progress, 97
    The Twelfth Session: Negotiations End, 98
    The Grievance Procedure, 99
    In Retrospect, 101

Chapter 7   103

Services and References

    Services, 103
    References, 105

1

Changing Relationships in Education

In 1966, there were thirty-three teacher strikes in the United States while the previous ten years produced only thirty-five.[1] The author of the article reporting these facts went on to say that there were eleven strikes in the first quarter of 1967 and that there is a "growing inclination among teachers and their organizations to take direct action (strikes)."[2] He concluded by predicting that teacher "strikes and stoppages" would probably increase in the next few years. It appears that his prophecy is proving to be correct, for in February, 1968, over 35,000 teachers belonging to the Florida Education Association staged a statewide walkout.

Teacher strikes were a phenomenon attributed only to the American Federation of Teachers a few years ago, but the Florida situation affirms the existence of a new posture in the National Education Association—a pos-

---

[1] Ronald W. Glass, "Work Stoppage and Teachers: History and Prospect," *Monthly Labor Review,* August, 1967, p. 43.
[2] *Ibid.,* p. 46.

ture which advocates strikes when they are necessary. We now find the AFT and NEA vying for supremacy in terms of the number of work stoppages or strikes in which the organization is involved.[3]

Along with the increase in strike activity, there has been an increase in the membership of teacher organizations, most notably the AFT which now approximates 150,000. There also has been an appreciable increase in the number of teacher bargaining units throughout the country.

It is common knowledge that teachers are more militant today than ever before, and the peaceful—even reverent—relationship which generally existed between the teacher and the administrator has changed drastically, especially since the beginning of this decade.

The literature which examines the teacher employment field is replete with articles describing this rising militancy as well as the general restiveness, and the growing gap between the teacher and the administrator. Several authors have suggested that the cause of these trends can be attributed primarily to the conditions of the times in which we live. Others ascribe the state of affairs to the lack of understanding and the rigidity of school administrators and board members. Some suggest that teachers are different today and seek more meaningful participating experiences in the decision-making functions of the school system. They conclude that the militant and organization route gives teachers an opportunity to enjoy this meaningful participation.

The problem is real, and is perhaps more widespread than is readily admitted. This chapter attempts to deal with a few of those factors which have contributed to the circumstances which explain today's changing employment relationships in education.

Bureaucratization

The American school was, at least until a few years ago, a conglomerate of small, static institutions which went about the business of educating children in a very personal manner. With the growth of our cities and the increasing mobility of people in our society, the school no longer could remain unresponsive to societal changes. The science revolution, the human-rights revolution, the economic revolution, the technology revolution, and the knowledge revolution have produced an *education revolution.*

---

[3]*Wall Street Journal,* February 13, 1968, p. 1.

To cope with changes and the rapidly varying rate of change, the American school system began to regroup and centralize. This centralizing process began as a reorganization into larger and less numerous districts and is continuing as a conscious effort to establish more varied and numerous special programs. All of this centralization and specialization has led to the development of a school bureaucracy. While bureaucracy is efficient when viewed in a Weberian sense, it also requires that rules and regulations become more impersonal, since it dictates non-discriminatory treatment. The kind of more effective utilization of resources which stems from bureaucracy, then, tends to mitigate against the benefits generally realized from the interpersonal interactions in the small organizational setting.

Bureaucracy tends to categorize teachers and to erode their uniqueness despite the growth of specialization. It almost demands that the teachers organize and band together in order to seek and achieve meaningful rewards, since their work denies them these benefits. Moreover, as meaningful participation in the schools' decision-making process is taken from the teachers' hands and given to a professional administrator, the most apparent avenue open for participation then becomes the teacher organization.

Bureaucracy also tends to alienate the teacher from the community since few teachers are hometown products; they tend rather to live in the suburbs, or they are anonymously buried in the large community.

This massive, new centralized approach indeed has contributed to the condition—a condition which is contagious and tends to be fanned by the psychology of "joining the band wagon" and being with the "in" group.

Today's Teachers

Yesterday's teachers were older, less educated, and more content with their environment than the teachers of today. Today's teachers are more educated; for example, they no longer allow someone else to choose their textbooks or develop the course content. Years ago, teachers clearly abdicated these kinds of responsibilities, often because they were not prepared to assume them. Not so today!

More and more young males are becoming teachers. These men are primary wage-earners and are anxious to contribute to the school system which is their main source of livelihood and means to advancement. They are challenging the system and are also challenging to the system.[4]

Since work is fairly abundant in our country today and since the teacher typically has an above-average education, there are other respectable occupations open to him. He, therefore, compares the benefits of a teaching job to his other alternatives and constantly agitates for change to make the teaching job yield rewards equal to others. If he succeeds, which apparently has been the case most often recently, he stays on, but if he is rebuffed, he exercises his option to choose another occupation. In either case, the school system is involved in rapid change.

The teacher is also a product of the times—times which point to rising expectations. These rising expectations must be fulfilled commensurately with the rest of society or the teacher rebels. Often, this rebellion manifests itself in the organization he joins. Obviously, the teacher of the 1960's has different needs and different motivations than his predecessor.

The Role of Behavioral Theory

The study of leadership and administration in modern organizations has stressed the importance of organization theory and behavioral analysis. The writings in the NSSE Yearbook of 1964 properly explain the importance of this new approach to administration in the educational setting.[5] Unfortunately, many school administrators have not yet accepted the behavioral approach and still more are not aware of it. While the adoption of the behavioral concept of management would not stop teacher militancy nor would it eliminate the need for an AFT or NEA, it no doubt would go a long way in helping administrators understand teachers and their desires. At the risk of doing these social scientists an injustice, the following is an attempt to explain in summary form the three main management schools and their development.

Until 1930, most school administrators adopted the scientific-management approach. These "managers" viewed employees as pieces of productive equipment. The most effective utilization of

---

[4]For a good analysis of these changes, see Robert E. Doherty and Walter E. Oberer, *Teachers, School Boards and Collective Bargaining: A Changing of the Guard* (Ithaca, New York: Cornell University Press, 1967), Chap. 1.

[5]Daniel E. Griffith, ed., *Behavioral Science and Educational Administration,* The Sixty-Third Yearbook of the Society for Study of Education, Part II (Chicago, Illinois: University of Chicago Press, 1964).

their skills in terms of physical considerations was felt to be the most essential feature of effective management. No human skills were needed in management—only rewards, punishments, and incentive. Emphasis was on "efficiency."

These disciples of F. W. Taylor were succeeded in the 1930's by The Human Relations School. Elton Mayo, *et al.*, studied people in groups within the organization. Simply stated, the disciples of this approach considered it sound management to attempt to understand the individual as a part of a group. Understanding the individual and treating him as a human was the chief concern, often at the expense of "efficiency."

In the last ten or fifteen years, the approach has been to recognize that there are organizational goals to be achieved. In attempting to meet these goals, a conscious effort to understand the individual and his needs is considered necessary. The ideal administrator attempts to satisfy the employees' needs which hopefully can be congruent with the organizational objectives.

Society and the Law

Since 1960, society has been changing rapidly. Perhaps the most important aspect of this change is that it has produced socially conscious, outward-directed youths. These youths, who are products of a healthy economy and who do not face the immediacy of an economic depression, are indeed different from the generation preceding them. They do, however, face the ever-present specter of global war and nuclear holocaust. The previous generation came out of a totally different past and can be described as inward-directed. The meaning of such a change in the attitudes of our young people is most important when it is related to the school, since it is clear that the school affects society. More realistically, however, and to a much greater extent, society affects the school.

This societal impact by the youth upon the school and its teachers has been great. The emphasis on growth, the trend to be involved in civil disobedience, etc., are affecting the teachers. They are seeking to make changes consistent with these new societal demands and values. Often, this leads to frustration and, subsequently, to teacher militancy and, ultimately, organization.

The other aspect deals with the law. Laws governing bargaining for employers in public employment are fast growing in number. To view teacher-negotiations law without due consideration of the growth in the public employment is unfair.

Public employment is the fastest-growing area in the world of work in the United States, and public-employee labor unions are also the fastest growing in their group (the AFT having the greatest growth rate of any American union). The general occurrences in public employment necessarily affect the teachers.

The public also is becoming aware that public bargaining is here to stay and that certain concessions must be made to this growing block of workers. Teachers have been cognizant of these developments and have used them to their advantage in terms of seeking salary increases and a voice through bargaining in an organizational framework.

Conclusion

The alienation of teachers from administrators and vice versa is rapidly developing throughout the country. The cause is not singular and the probabilities of stemming the tide seem remote. Teachers are seeking a greater voice in the school through organizational representation. It does not appear that they will once again seek individual bargaining in the school. Bakke has posed this question: "Is it inevitable and is it appropriate that teachers participate through collective representatives in joint determination and administration with superintendents and school boards of the terms of the employment relationship?"[6] His answer is Yes, and he goes on to say that it is now only a matter of which organization the teachers will choose to represent them in a given situation.

Since we have indicated that the collective negotiations relationship between administrators and teachers appears to be inevitable, it seems appropriate to consider what effect this process may have upon the school system, the teachers, and education generally. Charles S. Benson, Associate Professor of Education at the University of California at Berkeley, has come to these conclusions:

1. . . . collective negotiation . . . will serve to maintain an upward pressure on teachers salaries.

---

[6]E. Wright Bakke, "Teachers, School Boards and Employment Relations," *Employer-Employee Relationships in the Public School* (Ithaca, New York: New York State School of Industrial and Labor Relations, Cornell University, January, 1967), pp. 41-59.

2. ... collective negotiations is a force working for revitalization of Central City in America.
3. Collective negotiation will serve to revitalize the role of the public school teacher in America.[7]

While the evidence is not yet totally assembled, there is a greater consensus today than in previous years that collective negotiations will produce positive effects upon American education. These positive achievements should far outweigh the circumstances which may be detrimental.

---

[7]Charles S. Benson, "Economic Problem of Education Associated with Collective Negotiation," *The Changing Employment Relationship in Public Schools* (Ithaca, New York: New York State School of Industrial and Labor Relations, Cornell University, 1966), p. 2.

2

Organizational and Legal Structure of Collective Negotiations

The purpose of this chapter is to develop a framework for understanding the structural relationships involved in collective negotiations. By "structural relationships" is meant arrangements or ground rules developed through various state policies on collective negotiations and through agreements between school boards and employee associations. An attempt will be made here not to develop one model to be followed, but rather to outline the various structures developed in different states. In so doing, we will address ourselves to the following areas:

1. the employees' right to organize and bargain collectively and the duty to bargain;
2. recognition and the bargaining unit;
3. the scope of collective negotiations.

More specifically, we shall attempt to answer such questions as the following: Is the board of education legally required to recognize and bargain with employee organizations? Are there any guidelines regarding the areas that the board must be willing to discuss? What group will the board recognize and bargain with? Will it be only certified teaching personnel? Will it include ancillary personnel such as nurses, counselors, etc.? Will administrators be included? Will more than one organization be recognized? What method of recognition will be followed? Are there any restrictions on the conduct of actual negotiations? The answers to these and other questions should provide a framework for understanding the structure within which actual negotiations take place.

The Right to Organize and Bargain Collectively

As indicated elsewhere in this text, the right of teachers to further their interests as professionals and as employees is now generally conceded. State constitutions as well as the First and Fourteenth Amendments to the Federal Constitution are the legal bases. These two amendments guarantee the rights of assembly, association, and petitioning the government for redress of grievances. Many states have reasserted this right of public employees to form their own associations. Some states and municipalities have attempted to restrict public employees from joining any labor organization, but these are exceptions to the rule. Our discussion will proceed on the assumption that the right to self-organization is a fact of life.

Beyond the question of the right to self-organization is the problem of the rights and responsibilities of the local school board in dealing with an employee organization. Does the board have the right to forego its traditional unilateral decision-making in determining salaries, conditions of work, fringe benefits, etc.? Must it "consult" with the employee organization on these questions? Must it, in fact, "bargain" over these and other issues? Can the board legally sign a written negotiation agreement with its employee organization?

Two basic questions arise here: What is the board authorized to do? and what is it required to do with regard to collective negotiations? The traditional position, which now appears to be falling before new state laws and administrative decisions, was that governments and their subdivisions have the sovereign power to legislate and enforce the law within the limits of constitutional authority. The logic used concludes that collective negotiations would be a form of co-determination of matters that, legally, only the state or its agents may decide upon. In brief, this "sovereignty

Organizational and Legal Structure of Collective Negotiations 11

doctrine" holds that the state or its agents must set the terms and conditions for its employees unilaterally. To do otherwise would be an abdication of government responsibility, according to the "sovereignty" argument.

Present trends in federal and state policy regarding collective negotiations indicate that the sovereignty position is losing both its theoretical and practical support. Even where this concept is still accepted, it is being waived with the passage of state laws either allowing or requiring local school boards to consult with employee associations or actually negotiate with them on conditions of employment.

Another interpretation has been that government authority includes that of developing a policy regarding employee-employer relations and delegating or sharing the right to set conditions of employment. The degree of autonomy allowed local boards in negotiating with their employees now varies considerably by state. At present, there are eighteen states which have legislation authorizing or mandating collective dealings between government and some or all public employees. In seven states, school personnel are covered by separate detailed law[1] while in others they are included with other public employees. Several additional states now have commissions studying their legislative needs in this area. State laws, then, differ as to whether or not they are mandatory, employee coverage, administrative agency for the statute, type of representation provided for, etc. Table 1 gives a sample of the diversity of this legislation.

Returning to the authority and/or responsibility of the local board in its relationship with organized employees, the rules of the game vary from the approach used in Alaska authorizing but not requiring the board to negotiate, to a statute such as that in Rhode Island requiring the school board to negotiate, outlining and specifying bargainable issues and requiring that the agreement be in writing. It is becoming clearer each year that there is a strong trend toward a requirement on the part of the school board to negotiate. In states where the board has the option to negotiate or not, the growing strength of employee organizations will most likely make this option more academic than practical.

Most of the recent literature advancing guidelines for a "model" public-employee relations law stresses that government agencies

---

[1]California, Connecticut, Minnesota, Nebraska, Oregon, Rhode Island, and Washington.

TABLE 1
A Sample of State Public-Employee Relations Laws

State	Date	Coverage	Administrative Agency for Unit Determination and Elections	Type of Representation	Bargaining Unit Determined by	Representation Procedure	Includes Unfair Labor Practices
Minnesota	1967	Certificated teaching personnel except superintendents	Local school board	Proportional	Statute	School-board recognition	Yes
Nebraska	1967	Certificated public school employees	Local school board	Exclusive	Statute	Examination of membership list	Yes
New York	1967	All state employees	Public-Employment Relations Board	Exclusive	Local agency or, if appealed, by state board	By local agreement or state-supervised election	No
Rhode Island	1966	Certificated public school teachers; superintendents,	State Labor-Relations Board	Exclusive	Statute	Majority election by secret ballot	Yes

Organizational and Legal Structure of Collective Negotiations

California	1965	assistant superintendents, principals and assistant principals excluded	Proportional	—	Examination of membership lists	Yes
Oregon	1965	All certificated public school employees	Exclusive	District school board	Majority election	No
Washington	1965	Certificated public school personnel below rank of district superintendent	Exclusive	—	Majority election	No
Connecticut	1965	Certificated teaching personnel excluding superintendents	Exclusive	Impartial ad hoc agency	Majority election	No
Massachusetts	1965	Certificated professional personnel	Exclusive	Mass. Labor Commission	Majority by secret election or other suitable means	Yes
Michigan	1965	All city and county employees	Exclusive	Mass. Labor Commission		
		All public employees	Exclusive	Mich. Labor Mediation Board	Majority election	Yes

should be required to bargain in good faith rather than leaving the choice to do so optional. The authors agree strongly with this proposition.

A brief word is in order regarding the meaning of good-faith bargaining. In private-sector bargaining, this refers to the obligation of both parties to meet at reasonable times, be willing to make counterproposals, be willing to reduce the negotiated agreement to writing, etc. The state legislation in this area for the public sector again varies. However, the majority of states with legislation include the duty to bargain in good faith and the requirement that the agreement be in writing. It should be noted that both parties should be required to negotiate in good faith, not merely one side.

In summary, it is clear that school personnel do have the right of association and organization, and that the school board may be required by the state to bargain, may be specifically given the option to bargain, or that there may be no state guideline at all. In the absence of state statutes, school board and/or employees' associations have often requested rulings by state legal officials. Elaborate procedures for employee recognition and negotiations have been developed by the parties despite the fact that the state does not set ground rules. Possible procedures that might be used where the state offers no rules or guidelines will be discussed later in this chapter.

Recognition and the Bargaining Unit

One of the first questions to be resolved before collective negotiations can begin is, What group of employees is the school district bargaining committee to negotiate with? Will it be only with certified teaching personnel? Will it be with a group representing teachers, supervisors, and principals? Will there be separate negotiations with non-teaching personnel? Or shall they bargain as part of a group including professional personnel? Shall the organization proving majority support be given the right to bargain for all? Or shall different associations be allowed representation on the employee bargaining committee in proportion to their membership? Shall a vote be required to determine representation? If state law does not set guidelines, what procedure may a board follow? These are but a few of the issues involved in the question of recognition and bargaining unit determination.

To begin with, a bargaining unit may be defined as a group of jobs which are covered by the collective negotiations agreement.

There obviously must be agreement first on who is in the bargaining unit before negotiations can proceed. If there is to be an election to determine what organization shall represent the employees, a determination must be made as to who is eligible to vote. Those eligible voters will be the members of the bargaining unit.

As has already been indicated, the extent of the bargaining unit is often defined by state law. Rhode Island, for example, excludes superintendents, assistant superintendents, principals, and assistant principals.

The following are some of the possible types of bargaining unit:

1. certificated teaching personnel excluding those in a supervisory capacity such as principals, assistant superintendents, superintendents, etc.;
2. certificated teaching personnel including administrators;
3. all certificated personnel including ancillary personnel such as counselors, medical staff, etc.;
4. plant maintenance personnel in a separate unit.

As indicated in the previous section, the determination of the bargaining unit may be made by a state labor-relations board, by statute, by the local school district, or by a neutral party. An example of the use of a neutral is in Connecticut where the board and employee association agree on a neutral person or agency to settle the question of the appropriate bargaining unit. The latter method is often used where there is no guiding legislation.

Criteria for Determining an Appropriate Unit

What yardsticks have been used to justify one type of bargaining unit as opposed to another? Again, the experience varies by state. A community of interest among the employees to be included in the unit is often stressed. The extent of organization and any previous history of negotiation may be considered relevant. The desires of the employees could be a significant factor, or emphasis may be on the criteria of efficiency in negotiations. The Michigan Labor Mediation Board encourages the parties to reach mutual agreement on a bargaining unit with the restrictions that supervisors and non-supervisors not be in the same unit, that professional and non-professional people ordinarily should not be included in the same unit, etc. In the absence of mutual agreement by the parties, the mediation board may hold a hearing and render a decision.

The overriding criteria would seem to be the common employment interests of the employees, hence the frequent reluctance to include school custodians and teachers, for example, in the same unit. At the same time, there should be included some consideration of the effect of the unit on efficient school administration. Too many different bargaining units negotiating with the board can put a heavy strain on collective negotiations.

The positions of the two major employee associations in education differ on the question of whether teachers and administrators should be included in one bargaining unit. The National Education Association has advanced the view that administrators should be included, while the American Federation of Teachers strongly argues that teachers cannot effectively participate in a unit that includes their supervisors. In collective bargaining in the private sector, supervisors are excluded from federal legislative protection. As can be seen from state public-employee laws, there is some feeling along these same lines to separate administrators.

Types of Representation

There are two major types of representation that may be provided by state law or agreed to by the parties. These are exclusive representation and proportional representation as described below.

1. *Exclusive representation:* Under this arrangement, one organization represents all employees in a negotiating unit. If the organization can demonstrate majority support in the bargaining unit, it is then designated the negotiating representative for all members of that unit. This is the basic principle of federal law regulating labor-management relations in private industry. Even the employees who voted against that particular representative and do not join the association are represented by that group. The majority of state public-employee relations acts have provided for exclusive recognition to the organization chosen by a majority in the bargaining unit.

2. *Proportional representation:* This type of arrangement can be defined as one which includes more than one recognized employee organization where representation on the committee to negotiate with the school board is based on the proportion of school district employees represented by each organization. An example is the Minnesota law providing that there shall be a committee of five

teachers to negotiate with the board, and the committee makeup shall be, as nearly as possible, in proportion to the membership of each employee organization. California is another state using the proportional system.

Both the American Federation of Teachers and the National Education Association now support exclusive recognition, the NEA being a recent convert to this position.

Method of Recognition

Assuming that a bargaining unit has been agreed to and that it has been agreed that exclusive recognition will be the policy, what methods might the school board use to effectuate formal recognition? Once again state law varies, but there is one method that predominates; namely, the secret-ballot majority vote of employees. Depending on state law, such an election may be handled by the school district itself, by a state labor-relations board, or by a neutral party or organization. Under an exclusive recognition agreement, the organization receiving a majority of employee votes is certified as the negotiating representative for all in that bargaining unit.

In some states, the board may recognize an employee organization on the basis of examining certified membership lists or dues authorization cards. In California, for example, examination of membership lists is the representation method used.

A brief review of the procedure used in one state may be useful as an outline of one formal representation method. The following is the system recently adopted by New York State concerning all public employees. In New York, the school board may determine on its own whether an employee organization represents a majority, and if it finds that such a majority exists, it should grant recognition under the law. The question may go to the state public-employee relations board if the parties cannot agree on representation locally. The employer may petition the state board to handle the certification questions; the employee association may petition the state board if the school board does not respond to its request for recognition or if it is refused recognition; a competing employee association may petition the state board if it feels that the local school board should have recognized it instead of another group. The state board will process the petition if:

1. in cases where the employer has refused to respond, the employee organization can prove through membership cards, etc., a 30 per cent showing of interest;
2. in cases where review is sought of a local board's decision to voluntarily recognize an employee organization, a showing of 10 per cent is obtained. This also holds for an organization seeking to intervene in a representation proceeding.

For a bargaining representative to be certified without an election by the state board, there must be no competing group that has also shown substantial support. Specific percentages of support are spelled out by the board. As an example, if organization *A* proves support of 15 per cent of the employees, organization *B* must show 60 per cent to obtain certification without an election. All elections supervised by the state are by secret ballot, and a majority vote carries with it exclusive representation rights for a period of time specified in the law.

This one-state example may serve as a guideline for school districts lacking state ground rules. It illustrates some alternatives that might be adapted to the local situation.

In addition to the regulations of other states, the experience of school districts which have developed their own procedures may be useful to local districts without guidelines. For example, in Philadelphia, Pennsylvania, in 1964 the local board directed the superintendent to draw up a collective negotiations procedure for board approval.[2] A policy statement was developed on collective negotiations along with a plan of implementation. A representation procedure was developed with an impartial moderator certifying organizations for placement on the ballot, determining bargaining unit questions, etc. The election itself was supervised by the American Arbitration Association who later certified the results. The school board then recognized the group receiving a majority vote and extended exclusive representation rights to them.

The alternative methods of extending recognition should no longer be a mystery to those facing collective negotiations for the first time. Even in the absence of state guidelines, considerable experience has been built in a few short years, and the assistance of impartial organizations such as the American Arbitration Association can be of great help at reasonable cost.

---

[2]M. Lieberman and M. H. Moskow, *Collective Negotiations for Teachers: An Approach to School Administration* (Chicago: Rand McNally & Company, 1966), pp. 571-585.

Duration of Recognition

One further issue should be mentioned regarding the question of recognition. Once recognition is extended to an employee group, how long should this recognition remain in force? And how may representation elections be held? At stake here is the question of the stability of negotiation relationships and the protection of the rights of employees who may wish to challenge a group previously granted exclusive representation by the school board.

It is obvious that too many representation elections in a local situation can leave employee relations in chaos, and that it is in the interest of all parties that recognition be granted for a period long enough to promote stability but not so long that it impinges on the right of employees to challenge or change representatives.

Two types of limitation may be considered regarding the duration of recognition. One is usually referred to as an "election bar," the other as a "contract bar." These criteria, developed in private-industry collective bargaining, are now finding their way into public sector. In private industry, under the National Labor Relations Act, the election bar means that once an organization is certified by election as a bargaining agent, it is assured this recognition for one year. Normally, no other representation elections may be held in that bargaining unit for twelve months. Again, the rationale is to promote stability in employee relations. Under the same act, the contract bar provides that once an agreement has been negotiated between the parties, no representation elections will be held for the life of the contract up to a maximum duration of three years. Therefore, recognition without challenge is guaranteed for a minimum of one year and a maximum of three years.

One complication in the public sector should be noted. Budgetary deadline dates make it necessary that any representation elections be timed to leave a sufficient period for negotiations before budgets must be submitted. One suggestion has been made that election of teacher representatives be limited to once every two years to reduce this constraint imposed by budget submission and to promote stability.[3]

The election- and contract-bar concepts can now be found in some state legislation on public-employee relationships. The Michigan statute provides that no election will be held within twelve months after a valid election has been held. It further states that a

---

[3]Doherty and Oberer, *op. cit.*, p. 79.

valid negotiated agreement may constitute a bar to an election for a maximum period of three years.

Connecticut allows one election per school year while Rhode Island adds to the one-year rule a stipulation that any election must be at least thirty days prior to the expiration of any employment contract. The latter is an attempt to meet the budgetary deadline problem mentioned previously. Massachusetts law includes a contract bar, but rather than fixing a specific term, it leaves this question to the state labor-relations commission. A New Jersey study commission has recommended that legislation provide a bar for a specified period of time following an election.

Provisions regarding the duration of recognition can therefore be found in some state laws, but most states have not yet addressed themselves to this issue. It would certainly seem logical in the interests of employee rights and stable negotiations that a guarantee of at least one year of unchallenged certification be provided for.

We have attempted here to discuss the basic issues involved in recognition of bargaining representatives and the determination of a bargaining unit before analyzing the scope and content of negotiations. It should be obvious that these pre-bargaining issues and the manner in which they are handled can directly affect the character of the negotiations that follow. Badly handled, these issues can compound the difficulties that actual negotiations always present. Their resolution can significantly affect the relationship of the parties for years to come. An understanding of the state law within which the parties operate is essential, and in the absence of state guidelines, a thorough study by the parties of the issues presented here should have high priority.

The Scope of Collective Negotiations

Once having settled bargaining unit and representation questions, the parties are ready to develop some ground rules for negotiation. The following chapter will discuss the negotiation process itself, but since we are developing a framework for understanding the structure surrounding actual negotiations, it is necessary to examine the boundaries of collective negotiations. A fundamental issue to be faced regarding the scope of collective negotiations is, What areas will be considered subject to the process of bargaining? What issues are reserved to the school administration for unilateral decision-making? Another way of stating the issue is, What are the prerogatives or "management-rights" of the school board and its administrators which are not negotiable? Shall the board negotiate on salaries and fringe benefits only? Shall it negotiate on class size, rest periods, leaves of absence, curriculum development, etc.? What, then, will be the scope of collective negotiations?

Anyone seeking a definitive answer to the last question will be disappointed. The experience in private-sector bargaining is a case in point. The original Wagner Act of 1935 required private-industry employers to negotiate on wages, hours, and conditions of employment. The area of wages and hours was fairly clear. The difficult question concerned the meaning of "conditions of employment." Gradually, over the years, labor-board and court decisions have expanded the list of negotiable items until, today, valid questions are raised over such items as an employer's right to unilaterally subcontract work done by bargaining unit employees to outside firms. The trend has been to continually broaden the scope of bargaining.[4]

In public education, the issue of the scope of bargaining is perhaps even more pronounced than in the private sector. Unlike most labor unions in private industry, with their traditional emphasis on job security and economic benefits, the professional employee in education has already demonstrated a much broader interest in "how the business is run." The National Education Association has stated that negotiations should include all matters which affect the quality of the educational system. The American Federation of Teachers has stated that it would place no limit on the scope of negotiations. Some school boards, in the absence of any legislative guideline, react to the NEA and AFT positions by unduly narrowing the area of negotiations, fearing that "the teachers will take over."

At this unsettled stage of negotiations in public education, there are no agreed-upon criteria for the proper scope of negotiations. The pattern varies by state. California provides that school employers "shall meet and confer" with employee representatives as to all matters relating to employment conditions and employer-employee relations, including but not limited to wages, hours, and other terms and conditions of employment and as to the "definition of educational objectives, the determination of the content of courses and curricula, the selection of textbooks, and other aspects of the instructional program to the extent that such matters are

---

[4] It should be noted here that the duty to bargain does not mean capitulating to a specific demand. It does mean discussing the issue but does not imply a specific concession as such.

within the discretion of the public school employer or governing board under the law."[5] Other states frequently restrict negotiation to direct financial compensation and employment conditions. The new Minnesota law states that the board shall discuss "conditions of professional service, as well as educational and professional policies, relationships, grievance procedures, and other matters as apply to teachers."[6] In New Jersey, a study commission on public-employee relations recommended to the Governor and the legislature that "issues subject to mutual resolution are those relating to wages, salaries, working conditions, and other terms of employment. The scope of collective negotiations should not exceed the legal jurisdiction of appointing authorities of public employers or recommend legal policy."[7] With the exception of the right to strike and lockout, this commission recommended that "the broadest latitude for collective negotiations should be available to the public employers and employees."[8]

Meaningful negotiations require more than the narrowest possible interpretation of the scope of bargaining. Many school boards will find the transition from unilateral decision-making to bilateral determination a difficult and trying one. However, the school board that uses the principle of negotiating on as few issues as possible is probably defeating its own purpose in the long run. Again, negotiating an issue does not necessarily mean accepting the view of the other side regarding the content of that issue. Negotiators will undoubtedly find that the line between so-called administrative prerogatives and negotiable issues is difficult to define. Many students of employee relations have long felt that less emphasis on rights and more on problem solving eventually leads to a more satisfactory employee relationship.

Conclusion

At the beginning of this chapter, it was indicated that we would attempt to provide a framework for understanding the structural relationships involved in collective negotiations. We indicated that

---

[5]Doherty and Oberer, *op. cit.* p. 91.
[6]*Negotiation Research Digest,* National Education Association, Washington, D.C., September, 1967.
[7]Public and School Employees' Grievance Procedure Study Commission, Final Report to the Governor and the Legislature, State of New Jersey, January, 1968, p. 1.
[8]*Ibid.*

no attempt would be made to develop a model bargaining unit, recognition procedure, or boundary for the scope of negotiations. This would serve little purpose for the practitioner already operating under guidelines set by the state. For those school districts with a freer hand in developing a negotiation structure due to the absence of law, we have attempted to relate what some districts' policies have been and to point out the procedures already set up by some state laws that others may wish to adapt to their local situation and problems. We have left the structural arrangements for settling impasses for later discussion under the process of collective bargaining.

In determining a bargaining unit and delineating the scope of negotiations, it should be kept in mind that these problems cannot be divorced from actual negotiations or the administration of the agreement. For this reason, we have referred to collective negotiation as a process rather than a set of isolated problems.

As one observer of the collective negotiations scene has put it, "the key ingredients in negotiating are full and complete preparation, flexibility and attitude. To the extent any of these are inadequate, board-staff relations will suffer."[9]

In the last analysis, the purpose of collective negotiations is to provide a foundation for a stable, satisfactory working relationship in the school system and a better educational program in the district. A better understanding of the structure of collective negotiations can add immeasurably to the attainment of these goals.

---

[9]John Metzler, *A Journal of Collective Negotiations,* (Trenton, N.J.: State Federation District Boards of Education, 1967), p. 24.

3

Procedures and Techniques in Collective Negotiations

What Is Collective Negotiation?

Collective negotiation is an art. Concerned primarily with people, whose behavior is often unpredictable, it does not depend upon the formal rules, rigid performance, environmental control, and expected results of strict scientific procedure.

Davey, quoting John M. Clark, writes that collective bargaining (collective negotiation) is a "combination of psychology, politics, and poker."[1] This statement implies the lack of control exercised by either party. Moreover, it suggests that collective negotiation involves judgment, knowledge, and skills as well as attitudes, personality traits, and the dictates of particular situations.

Our discussion and treatment of the techniques in collective negotiations will not be centered about the mechanics, but rather about understanding the attitudes

---

[1] Harold W. Davey, *Contemporary Collective Bargaining,* 2nd ed. (Englewood Cliffs, N.J.: Prentice-Hall, Inc., 1959), p. 7.

and the interpersonal characteristics which are essential for successful negotiations. We must accept the basic premise that collective negotiation is not a game of winners or losers. It is, in fact, a constructive relationship for mutual problem solving based upon the mutual interests of the parties.

Teachers and administrators have goals and objectives in mind when they begin to negotiate. Each must be prepared to perceive the others' position with some degree of empathy and begin a process of accommodation where both participating groups conclude the formal negotiating session with benefits which are "livable" to the other party.

Too often, we view collective negotiation as a bilateral arrangement as opposed to a unilateral structure. More realistically, it is a multilateral arrangement with each of the bargaining organizations responsive to several elements within their own groups as well as the general public which watches the daily developments with great interest and concern.

Another important factor to keep in mind when referring to collective negotiation is that the process is a continuous one. The common notion is that negotiations take place annually and it is this annual crisis which must be dealt with on a singular basis. In reality, negotiations must be continuous in the sense that the negotiated agreement must be administered, interpreted, changed, augmented, and/or modified during the day-in day-out working relationship between teachers and administrators.

To summarize then:

1. Collective negotiation is more "art" than science, and the rules of predictability are difficult to establish and interpret;
2. The control over the outcome of negotiations does not rest in hands of either party or the "objective" observer;
3. Negotiations take place within groups (organizations) as well as between groups (organizations), and in all cases under the pressure of public interest and concern; and
4. Negotiation is not a crisis situation but a continuous process which evolves through the daily interchanges between teachers and administrators.

Why Collective Negotiations?

Since collective negotiations appear to be so difficult to predict (outcomes) and to describe, it might logically be asked, Why do parties negotiate? Obviously, because it is the desired procedure by one or both parties and often it is legally required.[2] Another important consideration is, Why study or learn about collective negotiation since the rules are flexible and the lack of uniformity is such that it is useless as an area of study? This question requires a lengthy reply and explanation.

Collective negotiations do differ from time to time, place to place, and when the actors involved are changed. Even where the actors don't change, uniformity of action, conduct, and outcomes is lacking. Other factors which contribute to the lack of stability are: the school districts themselves, the economics of the locale and the nation, the social and cultural characteristics of the community, the law or the lack of law, the financial resources of the school, etc. The list is perhaps inexhaustible and what is more important, it is impossible to keep one or more of the above conditions constant and, by way of controlled experimentation, determine and predict outcomes. *Nevertheless, by inspecting the process and procedure (or the framework) which is usually employed in bargaining or negotiating, it is possible to have a greater understanding of the phenomenon.*

It is often heard that since negotiation is a people phenomenon, it is then logical to study only people and consequently omit the study of collective negotiations per se. This can be rejected by the experience in private industry and the growth of industrial relations as an area of study. Collective negotiation *is* the study of people acting together in groups where they are concerned about common problems affecting their working life and environment.

How to View Collective Negotiations—Some Structures

Lieberman and Moskow borrowed liberally from Chamberlain and Kuhn when they discussed three structures of bargaining or negotiating.[3] They refer to negotiating arrangements as either (1) economic, or marketing arrangements, (2) professional arrangements or (3) problem-solving arrangements.

The economic or market arrangement simply stated observes the structure as an economic relationship in which the teacher performs a service, is paid for it, with teacher and administrator

---

[2]It should be emphasized here that the absence of legislation should not necessarily preclude negotiations. A review of Chap. 2 provides a more detailed analysis of this question.

[3]Lieberman and Moskow, *op. cit.,* pp. 7-10. See also Neil W. Chamberlain and James W. Kuhn, *Collective Bargaining,* 2nd ed. rev. (New York: McGraw-Hill, Inc., 1965).

both using economic or market forces to secure their best position. Under this arrangement, bargaining is not continuous, communications are meager, and the relationships between teacher and administrator are indeed strained.

The professional arrangement (referred to as the "management approach" by Chamberlain and Kuhn) stresses that the administration and management of the school can be mutually performed by the administrator and the professional teacher in those areas where the teacher has concern, professionalism, and expertise. This approach expands the teacher's interests beyond those basic economic issues and brings him into focus in a more "professional" manner.

The problem-solving arrangement (or cooperative approach) goes beyond the economic relationship and the professional or accommodating relationship. This arrangement assumes that of several problems to be dealt with in the school, they can best be managed by teachers and administrators working harmoniously together. Indeed, this is the most mature level, although most often it is idealistic. Unfortunately, in most instances, schools do not operate at such a level, and in cases where teachers organize and band together to achieve greater participation in the decision-making function, the arrangement between them and administrators remains at the market level or at best develops to the professional level.

Negotiations, Ritualism, and the Individual

Several times we have referred to collective negotiation as a people phenomenon and in the same breath talk about organizations. To view the negotiating relationship as one existing between two organizations would be to avoid and omit the people within the organizations. The workings of the organizations will be examined more closely later on, but at this point our primary concern is people.

The bargaining process is one in which the actors involved have some idea of the outcomes before negotiations begin. Why then—if they know or can be reasonably sure of the outcome—do they bargain? One answer is the need for ceremony or ritual. Our society demands that we carry on a certain amount of ceremony or ritual; for example, our television wild west programs always show the Indians donning war paint and drinking hard liquor before the battle; they never fight before preparation or ceremony. We can predict what the speaker will say on graduation day (high school), and we know what to expect of the public officials who speak on Veterans Day or Independence Day. Yet, the ritual must be held. Likewise, the bargaining or negotiating process provides a mechanism for the ritual. It is the expected ceremony for those actors involved and it must be held.

We often think we know what to expect since we know the school budget, or the appropriated budget, or the reaction of the taxpayers and board members to teacher demands; but, in fact, we don't always know what to expect! Sometimes there is a miscalculation by both groups which can be cleared up in the negotiating process. The New York City situation a few years ago is a good example. The teachers demanded wage increases and the school administrators claimed no funds were available. After much discussion and great difficulties, the mayor of the city entered the dispute and approximately ten million dollars was "found" for the teachers.

The leaders of the teacher organization need the hard negotiating session to demonstrate their usefulness. If the benefits conceded to a leader of a teacher organization through "hard bargaining" were "given" without negotiations, then the usefulness of both the teacher organization and its leader would be challenged. In such a case, they would desire more benefits rather than a resolution of the dispute or a collapse of the teacher organization. Likewise, the administrator often needs the negotiating session and the pressure placed on him by the teacher organization to influence others on his team to change their stance. Therefore, it seems to follow that the bargaining ceremony or ritual has organizational as well as institutional importance.

If one accepts the notion that teacher organizations arise because of the lack of individual teacher participation in the organizational decision-making scheme, and that the loss of communication between teachers and administrators is due to this lack of participation, then it follows that collective negotiation is a channel to allow for more communications and greater participation. It is true that in organizations which are autocratic, communications channel downward only. The organization of teachers, then, often serves as a vehicle to channel information upward and to keep the flow and exchange of information and ideas current and open.

One last consideration is the function which the negotiations process performs when the relationship between administrators and the teacher organization is stale. The negotiations process allows for "airing-out" of grievances and for a general "house cleaning." It also strengthens the hand of leaders of both groups if they resist the demand of the other based upon a sound defense of a tenable and justifiable position. Occasionally, the organizations go on for years without resolving differences or considering them. Hard bargaining by negotiating sessions helps to meet these problems head on.

Preparation for Negotiations

While the general rules of traditional collective bargaining as they relate to negotiations are applicable to the teacher arena, some specifics regarding the uniqueness of the school setting are important to remember. The school is usually on annual budget and likewise are the teachers' contracts. (Employees in private industry usually do not have a written contract but, in effect, there is indeed a contract although the duration is not as specific as in public education.) These annual features are restrictions which need careful attention. Another factor to keep in mind relates to the amount of dollars budgeted for teacher salaries and the public concern. The public is vitally interested in the negotiations since it is their tax dollars and their children's education at stake. The legal right to strike is not afforded public employees in the United States, and, of course, it is a consideration which must be viewed in both a legal and a real sense.

Other considerations include the presence or absence of legislation, the existence of past negotiating sessions, the type or types of teacher groups present, and the administrator's attitude towards negotiations.

Let us consider the preparation in situations where either there have been no negotiations in the past or the teachers desire negotiations and have not selected an organization to represent them. In addition, let us assume that there is no state law allowing bargaining and that there are no restrictions on public bargaining.

With these conditions in mind, we may consider preparations in the traditional collective bargaining sense which may be considered an "AFT" approach, or we may consider the "NEA" approach as outlined by a state teachers' association.

Preparations for Negotiations for Management and the Employee Organization

The traditional view for collective bargaining perhaps has been best explained by Davey. The following may be considered the steps generally followed by management in preparation for negotiations:

1. Thorough study of the present contract with a view to discovering sections that require modification.
2. Close analysis of grievances in order to discover defective or unworkable contract language, and to indicate future employee organization demands.
3. Frequent conferences with (principals and supervisors) for the dual purpose of better training of supervision in contract administration and receipt of intelligence as to how the contract is working out in practice.
4. Conferences with (representatives from other districts) in the area who have contracts with the same employee organization for the purpose of exchanging viewpoints and anticipating future demands.
5. Use of attitude surveys to test the reactions of employees to various sections of the contract that (the board) may feel require change or modification.
6. Informal conferences with local employee organization leaders to discuss the operational effectiveness of the contract and to send up trial balloons on . . . ideas for change at the next negotiations.
7. Study of a commercial reporting service on labor relations matters for the purpose of keeping abreast of recent developments that may affect future contract negotiations.
8. Collection and analysis of economic data on issues likely to be of importance in the next negotiations.
9. Study and analysis of arbitration decisions under the current contract with a view of formulating proposals for changed contract language at the next negotiations. . . .[4]

The list below may be classified as a grouping generally followed by labor unions:

1. Careful analysis of the current contract to note any flaws from the employee organization's standpoint that may form the basis for new demands.
2. Careful analysis of the nature and source of grievances as a guide for future negotiation proposals and as a means of discovering imperfections in the current instrument.

---

[4]Davey, *op. cit.,* pp. 102-103. (with permission of publisher)

3. Use of the grievance procedure as a means of testing new contract language to see whether it is satisfactory or may require further modification in future contracts to accomplish the employee organization's objective.
4. Close analysis of arbitration decisions under the existing contract as a basis for formulating demands for changed language, new contract sections, or contract deletions.
5. Periodic conferences with local organization leaders for the dual purpose of improved contract administration and receiving ideas from those in the front lines of the grievance process as to how the contract is working out on a day-to-day basis.
6. Careful comparison of the current contract with other agreements in the area held by rival organizations or other locals of the same organization as a source of ideas for improvement.
7. Informal conferences with management as a device for sounding out potential management reactions to various proposals that may be in the employee organization's future expectations.
8. Holding of one or more local employee organization membership meetings considerably in advance of contract negotiation time for the specific purpose of receiving rank-and-file suggestions for demands.
9. Collection and analysis of economic data on salaries and other issues likely to be important.
10. Educating the membership in advance as to the basic content and rationale of the principal bargaining demands to insure united support.[5]

For an NEA-integrated approach to the entire negotiations process from preparation time until completion, the following items are a summary prepared by the Iowa State Education Association:

I. Summary (In form of typical sequence of events)
   A. Association requests recognition for negotiation.
   B. Association becomes spokesman for professional staff.
   C. Record center established.
   D. Association adopts policy which requires school-board action.

---

[5]*Ibid.*, p. 104. (with permission of publisher)

Procedures and Techniques in Collective Negotiations

E. Executive committee informs membership.
F. Executive committee plans strategy.
G. President appoints negotiation team.
H. Negotiation team plans tactics.
I. Letter of transmittal and document of preliminary submission to open negotiation.
J. Negotiation team meets with administration as directed by school board.
K. Negotiation team negotiates with board.
L. Letters of confirmation have been used following all meetings with administration and board.
M. Memo of agreement or letter of confirmation used when agreement reached.
N. Board incorporates the agreement into the policies of the school district.[6]

Who Should Negotiate?

In a local organization of teachers, the leader of that organization should either appoint a negotiating committee or conduct elections to determine the membership of such a committee. The negotiating committee should be comprised of a representative cross section of the teachers in the bargaining unit. For example, it might include high school, junior high, and elementary teachers or others such as special-education teachers, or ancillary personnel such as guidance counselors. The size of the group, however, should not be too large for then it becomes unmanageable; perhaps a maximum number might be six.

The group should elect a chairman. The chairman should be one who is articulate and forceful and who can speak for the group. The selection of a chairman is an important step—he should be a respected, even-tempered individual who can be trusted with the responsibility required of him.

For the school system, the spokesman should be the superintendent or his designated official. If not the school superintendent, such a person might be a personnel officer, an assistant superintendent, or any other member of the administrative team who has the capabilities and the authority to speak for school management.

---

[6]*Guidelines for Professional Negotiations in Iowa* (Des Moines, Iowa: Iowa State Education Association, September, 1967), pp. 27-28.

Special Note on the Role of Attorneys and Board Members

While consultation with an attorney might be desired and/or necessary for both the employee and employer group, the authors suggest that the negotiations should be left to the parties. Legal advice is perhaps essential, but the overindulgence in the use of outside legal assistance by the parties tends only to retard negotiations. Remember, the objective is to achieve a settlement which is simple, workable, understandable, and acceptable.

Of course, the board is concerned for its school, its administrator, and its teachers. Nevertheless, the board should not become involved in negotiation unless the board's confidence in its administrators is shaken. The board's chief role is to provide policy guidelines to the administrators prior to negotiations in order that the administrator have a reference point to guide him through the sessions. As a policy-making group, the board should only administer policy and let administrative responsibilities rest with the administrator.

The question as to what posture the board will adopt is important. Should a market structure or a management structure prevail? Only a consensus of the board can deal with this question. In this connection, the board may have certain "requests" that they seek from the employee organization, and they can use the pre-bargaining meeting with its administrators to explore these items.

How Should Negotiation Proceed?

Before the board and teacher negotiating committee meet with each other, they should have their own internal meeting to determine their strategy. The teacher committee should draw up a list of issues taken from the several requests and meetings with the teachers. They must distill these issues down to a workable number, establish priorities, and make the issues fairly reasonable. The teacher committee should not seek demands which are considered "way out" or "blue-sky proposals." If this group has done its homework, it will have checked area wages, competing school salaries, and the other fringes as well as working conditions. It will have a base from which to argue and evidence or facts to support its case.

The school administrator and his team will likewise prepare

their case and should muster evidence which is most beneficial to support it.

Each group will probably have internal meetings prior to negotiations and meetings with other state, regional, or national groups. For example, the teacher organization may meet with other local organizations, state organizations, and national groups. The school administrator will discuss his position with other administrators within his system and in other systems, and even with those associated with a state or national association to which he may belong.

Formal talks usually begin two to three months before contract expiration or renewal time or the period when individual negotiations are customarily started.

These first meetings are not serious; they are probing meetings where little seems to be accomplished. However, they are especially helpful if the parties use them to assess the other party position. They may be likened to the first few rounds in a typical heavyweight boxing match where the fighters look for each other's strengths and weaknesses and "test out" these areas.

Finally, as the deadline approaches, the talks become more lengthy and more earnest.

Listed on the following pages are some guidelines for the negotiating sessions themselves.

1. *Mutual Respect*—Successful and careful negotiations are predicated upon mutual respect. If this is lacking, then suspicion and difficulty will plague negotiations and the resultant agreement. To win mutual respect the following are needed:
    a) *Knowledge*—Parties should avoid negotiating or administering the agreement without adequate preparation. Facts must be secured and arguments organized before meaningful negotiations can take place.
    b) *Skill*—Parties must be able to communicate and to persuade; that is, skill in interpersonal relations is essential. Be willing and *able* to listen.
    c) *Judgment*—Parties need the ability to account for the future implications of their proposals and the ability to judge counterproposals objectively.
    d) *Courage*—Arguments must be expressed forcefully at times, as well as persuasively. Most people will respect the convictions of a person who is willing and able to defend them.

2. *Problem-Oriented Negotiations:*
   a) The worst ingredient in negotiating is the development of personality clashes. To avoid this pitfall, always permit the other party an opportunity to save face when he accepts a proposal. Avoid any temptation to belittle another's argument or to make rash statements.
   b) Start negotiations from areas of common agreement before attempting to resolve areas of dispute.
   c) Search out areas of mutual benefit as much as possible.
   d) Treat areas of dispute as problems to be mutually resolved rather than points to be debated.

The above elements are concerned with an overall approach to the negotiations process. The following sections describe in more specific detail those elements which are essential for a successful negotiations relationship.

The basic objective in collective negotiations, and this includes both negotiations and contract administration, is to reach agreement. Unfortunately, there are teacher representatives and administrators who think of collective negotiations as some kind of trial by combat or formal debate. Such an attitude raises serious obstacles to the development of a constructive teacher organization-administration relationship. To facilitate a sound agreement in negotiations and workable resolutions to problems, the following elements are suggested:

1. *The "Yes Habit":*
   Start discussions from areas of common agreement rather than from an obviously controversial area. Secure a basis of agreement on which to build and you will find that subsequent favorable accommodations are more easily reached on disputed issues.
2. *Assume Acceptance:*
   Do not indicate that you lack confidence in the reasonableness or acceptability of any major proposal. If you indicate in any way that your proposal might be turned down, it probably will be.
3. *The Forced Choice:*
   It is often difficult to reach a decision. Generally, the more that rides on a given decision, the more difficult it is to reach. The "forced choice" is an attempt to ease the burden of a weighty decision by offering a choice between

alternatives. There are many situations where two alternatives may be of relatively equal value. Avoid, as much as possible, offering a choice between *something* and *nothing*.

4. *Allow for Face-Saving:*

    It never hurts to be gracious. If you win a point, credit the other party for his sincerity and fairmindedness. To gloat and chortle over minor "victories" may make it impossible for the other side to offer reasonable compromises without resentment and embarrassment.

5. *The Burden of Proof:*

    In the nature of traditional collective bargaining, the teacher organization is the moving party. The moving party inherently tends to assume the burden of proving its case. This is as it should be, but the other party is likewise obliged to explain the reasons for rejecting any demand or proposal.

6. *Explain, Discuss, Persuade—Don't Plead:*

    In collective negotiations, there should not be any pleading or begging by either party. Be quick to demonstrate respect and courtesy and be equally quick to demand the same decorous consideration.

7. *Cite the Advantages of Your Proposal to the Other Party:*

    While this approach can be easily overdone, it happens with some frequency that the employee organization proposal carries some important advantages for the school district, just as a proposal from the administration may carry advantages for the teachers. Where these benefits to either party are significant, they serve as a proper additional factor in support of your case.

8. *Keep Discussions Problem-Oriented Rather Than Personality-Centered:*

    By far the most fruitful atmosphere for reaching sound agreements is the recognition by both parties of mutual interest in solving problems of common concern. The greater the degree of objectivity that can be developed, the more constructive the relationship. It often takes considerable time to overcome personality-centered clashes which mar the relationship. Collective negotiation at its best is a systematic, conscientious search for answers that work— answers which maximize satisfactions on the job while minimizing frustrations. The collective negotiations process certainly has shortcomings as a means of resolving conflicting interests in the school. It happens, however, to be much superior to any known alternative for adjusting differences in our society. It is worth the continuing effort by men of honorable intent to improve its functioning. In addition to constant improvement of your knowledge and skill, successful negotiations require patience and good will.

Negotiations in Relation to the Teacher Organization, the Board, and the Public

The negotiations process does not occur in a vacuum—it goes on in a fish bowl. Nevertheless, sometimes those outside of the fish bowl do not see all that is going on inside and, often, what they do see or hear is distorted. While secrecy is dangerous, the overexposure of too much information may be harmful to the resolution of problems. Therefore, some general rules might be followed in dealing with the teacher organization, the board, and the public.

Negotiations in Relation to the Membership for the Teacher Organization

1. *Preliminary Activities:*
   a) Creating the proper climate for negotiations by reminding members of the fact that they are the employee organization and the committee will be as effective as they make it;
   b) Assembling facts for negotiations such as the general economic situation; what is happening generally in education; what is happening in the same area; the idea of holding regional or district meetings of members to discuss negotiations and, in turn, making these meetings meaningful to the rest of the membership; getting facts from the members concerning old problems in administering the agreement—both won and lost—serving as indications of problems not covered by the existing contract;
   c) Anticipating the school district's proposals and counterproposals and preparing members for what the administrators will probably be saying.

2. *Election or Selection of Bargaining Committee:*
    There may be a standing committee or one developed for each negotiation. Generally, some overlapping of experience has advantages.
3. *Preparation of Actual Proposals:*
    Two suggested methods:
    a) Working up *clauses* in exact contract language. This offers the solution as well as the problem, and it is possible that devotion to language or to an exact solution may hinder agreement;
    b) Presenting the *problem* with a generalized suggestion for its solution. This allows more freedom for bargaining with less initial bickering on language. A combination of both methods might be advisable.

    Work up suggestions from the membership, relate national or state proposals to the local situation, and be sure that all proposals have a firm local basis. There is also something to be said for bringing the members together to pass on final proposals; it can help build enthusiasm and support and keep the teachers informed of what is going on.
4. *Dealing With the Administration's Proposals:*
    Prepare members for the probable school-district approach and arguments. While the exact position taken by the board and the administrators is difficult to assess, there can be some trends and arguments which may be anticipated. These should be discussed with the membership and a strategy developed.
5. *While Negotiations Are in Process:*
    Keep in close touch with the membership through progress reports. This gives the teachers a feeling of participation and emphasizes the importance of support for the committee. Reports on lack of progress have the same significance as those on progress. Some ways of keeping in touch include regular and special meetings; talks by committee members, officers, and active members; leaflets in the teachers lounge; news stories, ads, and radio. The idea of developing a school committee with representatives from each department to serve as a reporting and advisory and contact body is sound.

6. *When Negotiations Are Completed:*

In the report to the membership on what has been agreed to, a frank presentation is advisable both on principle and to avoid future troubles. Excessive and unrealistic proposals made initially by the teacher organization can present problems at this stage of the process. If certain proposals were not obtained, it may be well to explain why in terms of the larger situation. Factors limiting success may be reviewed to give members a better understanding of what is involved; factors contributing to success should be reviewed for the same reason.

General plans for the future in light of what has been achieved in the present may be reviewed to impress members with the fact that bargaining is a continuous process. In fact, there is value in setting up a system whereby active members can keep a record of suggested changes for the future based on the experience under the existing contract. Many good ideas are lost for lack of a system.

Finally, it is worth stressing the importance of making the new agreement work—to keep it a living document.

Negotiations: The Administrator's Relationship with the Board and his Fellow Administrators

1. *Preliminary Activities:*

In creating the proper climate for negotiations the administrator must discuss the bargaining situation with the board and secure accurate information and complete understanding that the negotiating role is the primary concern of the administrator. The administrator's effectiveness as a respected leader rests upon his authority in the negotiating session.

To secure this posture, the administrator must have the facts and present them to the board; describe the school situation as it relates to teacher morale, turnover, competitiveness of the salary structure, experience in the past, and the schools' capabilities in meeting teachers' demands within the community tax structure and revenue-producing abilities.

2. *Preparation of Actual Proposals:*

If the administrator accepts the notion that the teacher organization is the aggressor organization, he has the following alternatives:

Procedures and Techniques in Collective Negotiations 41

a) He can react to the teacher contract proposal. The advantage of this position is that it gives the administration flexibility and a chance to prepare—to discuss the proposal with the board. On the other hand, the "waiting game" can be dangerous since the "demands" may be too difficult to deal with and the die has been cast by the teacher organization.

b) He can develop a list of his own issues or a proposal which gives him the element of initiative—thus, making him the aggressor. In such a case, a position of bargaining strategy may give him some leverage with the teacher organization. However, this posture is sometimes more rigid and difficult to make stronger once a direction has been indicated.

Whichever posture is adopted, the administrator must get the board's endorsement and keep board members informed as to the progress of the situation.

3. *While Negotiations Are in Progress:*

The administrator should keep in close touch with the board of education and his own staff. Consistency of action and understanding of the state of progress is important. In addition, the same element of participation that is essential to the teachers is also relevant to the administrative team. The ways in which the channels of communications can remain open include regular meetings, informal and personal meetings, memoranda, and written communications.

4. *When Negotiations Are Completed:*

A full report to both the administrative team and the board is essential. Since the administrators must be knowledgeable and have the responsibility of carrying out the agreement, they should be aware of its contents. Prior to their acceptance of the contract, however, the board must approve of the agreements. The ultimate responsible agent to the public is indeed the board.

If some of the agreements are borderline, they must be fully considered and weighed by the board. Remember, the agreement at the conference table must ultimately be written up and finally formalized after approval by both the board and the teacher organization as a body. While the conference table agreement is probably the general understanding realized, it must ultimately be passed on by the higher authorities. The administrator should point out to the board the ramifications of the agreement as they will affect the entire school system in the future—the teaching staff, the financial structure, recruitment, education, the student body, the community, the tax structure, and the physical facilities.

Contract Negotiations in Relation to the Community

Since negotiations of a public institution are the concern of the general public and the process involves the public, it is essential that the following procedure be kept in mind by both parties:

1. The parties have a responsibility to the community to let their positions be known and to give reasons in support of their positions. This is especially true in the school-bargaining situations, since the school is such a visible public institution. The citizens look for it; they want assurances and arguments they can accept.
2. The employee organization and the administration—if they do engage in publicity during negotiations—have a similar responsibility to report to the community on progress or lack of progress.
3. In the event that negotiations are really difficult, some indication of this should reach the community so that an impasse does not catch the community unaware.

What to Negotiate

In the private sector, wages, hours, and working conditions are negotiable items by law. By and large, the laws in the various states allow for the same general consideration for teacher negotiations. However, some states such as California have statutes which specify particular items which can be bilaterally determined.

It is clear that as negotiations mature and develop, the penetration into so-called "managements rights" areas by employee organizations becomes greater. The same is true in the school area. Therefore, it should be expected by teachers and administrators that the scope of the items to be negotiated will increase as negotiations evolve and develop.

While the economic consideration makes the headlines and is, indeed, important, several studies and surveys continue to point out that teachers consider other factors as important if not more so. Consequently, the assessment of priority of items is not uniform, and the items to be negotiated vary by school system.

Listed below are but some of the items which are often placed on the negotiating table:

- Grievance procedure (including arbitration)
- Salaries
- Teaching hours and teaching loads
- Class size
- Use of specialists
- Non-teaching duties
- Teacher employment and assignment
- Transfers
- Vacancies and promotions
- Summer school and night school
- Teacher evaluation
- Discipline of teachers
- Salary schedules for the school year
- Individual teacher contracts
- Teacher facilities
- Use of school facilities
- Sick leaves
- Temporary leaves of absence
- Extended leaves of absence
- Sabbatical leaves
- Student control and discipline
- Protection of teachers
- Health insurance
- Retirement
- Professional development and educational improvement
- Textbooks
- Dues deduction
- Duration

The Written Agreement

The negotiating sessions should culminate in a written agreement. An agreement can be a simple document or a lengthy, legal one. What is important about the agreement is not its language, but rather the intent of the parties when it was drafted and how they will attempt to live with the agreement. There is no universal cookbook for writing an agreement, but Marceau has given some excellent general guidelines.

The ideal union contract, while difficult to create, is not difficult to envision. It would have the following characteristics:

1. When a reader wants to learn what the rule is, on any subject the contract covers, an index or table of contents will quickly refer him to the page the rule is on.
2. When he turns to the page, he will find a prominent caption showing the place on the page where the rule appears.
3. Everything that the contract has to say about the subject

will be said (or at least referred to) at that place. The reader may be referred to other sections for details, but the rule set forth will be reasonably complete.
4. The language setting forth the rule will be subject to only one possible interpretation.
5. The language will be so clear-cut that the reader can easily tell whether it applies to the existing facts. "6 A.M.," for example, is preferable to "dawn."
6. The rule set forth will accurately state what the parties have agreed on.
7. The rule will be stated simply enough to be understood by the people who can be expected to use the contract.
8. The rule will be short enough so that those people can grasp it readily, and possibly remember it.
9. The rule will be adaptable to changing conditions. That is, despite the normal changes that can be expected to occur, the rule will continue to meet the desires of the parties, and will require amendment only when a particularly far-reaching change occurs.
10. When the rule must be amended, it will be possible to amend it without changing many other parts of the contract.[7]

Administering the Agreement

The heart of collective negotiations is not the negotiating sessions. It is, rather, the daily administration of the agreement. The more mature the bargaining relationship, the greater the reliance upon the administration aspects of the relationship.

In private industry, the administration of the agreement is referred to most commonly as the grievance procedure. The grievance procedure is a vehicle used for interpreting what was written in the agreement by joint meetings of employees and the employer. The employer usually listens to an employee appeal which follows steps up the hierarchy of both organizations until the dispute is settled to the satisfaction of both parties. If there is no settlement, the dispute is usually submitted to an impartial third party for arbitration.

---

[7] LeRoy Marceau, *Drafting a Union Contract* (Boston: Little Brown and Company, 1965), pp. xxvii-xxviii.

The grievance or appeal might be a contract violation, misinterpretation, a violation of law, or a violation of established school policy or practice.

Grievance processing or appeals procedures may be handled in a very legal sense or in a clinical manner. If either or both parties to a contract insist that the other perform to the letter of the law, or the agreement, or the policy of the employing organization, then grievance handling is considered "legalistic." If such a track is followed by one party, it can be assured that the other party will likewise insist upon the same arrangement. Such action makes for a stilted, formalized arrangement with great friction between the parties and the use of attorney and legal means to resolve problems.

The other approach (clinical) demands that the parties be fair and live by the intent of the agreement, the law, or the policies. While misinterpretation is still possible and does occur, the flexible arrangement between the parties allows for a more reasonable resolution of problems for the mutual benefit of all concerned. The arrangement between employees and employers is a continuous one. It calls for accommodation and cooperation. While it is true that disputes between them will arise and that they should be handled indiscriminately, fairly, and systematically, it is also true that the relationship is constantly changing—it is dynamic, and any meaningful and helpful dealings must have enough flexibility to deal with the constant change.

In making appeals or grievances, teachers should remember to:

1. process only those which have merit;
2. not process grievances for political reasons;
3. spell out exactly the elements in dispute; for example, the parties involved, when and where the event occurred, and if it was a contract violation;
4. not trade a grievance of one teacher for that of another;
5. not let the grievance procedure become a "griping procedure";
6. not stall in handling appeals;

It would be well for school administrators to remember to:

1. handle grievances fairly;
2. not try to trade grievances;

3. use the grievance procedure as an index for teacher content or discontent;
4. use the grievance procedure as a communications vehicle;
5. use the grievance procedure as a means of assessing their own fairness or effectiveness as administrators; and
6. use the grievance procedure to build a relationship with the teacher organization.

If the parties to a collective agreement attempt to be empathic and realize that the relationship is continuous, calling for constant accommodation, then the negotiations process and the resultant collective agreement ought to prove meaningful.

4

The Language of Collective Negotiations

Quality in Communications

In any social setting, the process of communications is an integral part of the total scene. It is necessary to understand that the quality of communications of the parties in collective negotiations may be critical to the final outcomes of the negotiating process. Therefore, both parties should be particularly aware of *the quality of their speaking* and *the quality of their listening*. Both of these important communications elements can make a positive or negative contribution in the negotiations setting.

In speaking, the quality can be gauged by clarity of purpose, ability to assess the situation, use of positive language, avoidance of negative words, and reaching common understanding of the meaning of words and phrases that are appropriate to the occasion.

A plainness of words should be actively sought and achieved. Ideas should not be hidden by ponderous or obscure language. In referring to a "spade," do not call it an "instrument for excavation."

There are phrases that can be classified as positive. Other phrases are essentially negative. Some examples are:

Positive	Negative
That is reasonable	You are slanting the facts
Can we reach consensus	
We agree	You don't understand
We will concede . . . however,	You are wrong
	You are prejudiced
Let me clarify	That isn't true
Let's examine in another light	You don't know what you're talking about

When using positive words, the individual is practicing good faith in negotiations. When negative phrases are continuously used, a hostile atmosphere may result, undermining good-faith negotiating.

Words and Phrases Defined

One of the practices that should be adopted by negotiators is to come to some agreement on a commonly accepted definition of words or phrases. If semantic problems can be eliminated or minimized, the reaching of agreement on issues can be expedited.

In the realm of education, the language of labor-oriented and association-oriented organizations differs in many instances, although there are people who claim that there is no difference in the words "bargaining" and "negotiating" or in "demands" and "issues." If there is ever a merger of the labor-oriented and association-oriented teacher organizations, we may see the adoption of a common set of words and phrases in collective negotiations.

It should be clearly understood that words and phrases have "arbitrary significance." Miller points out that "words signify only what we have learned that they signify."[1] Berlo puts the same idea into another light when he asserts that, ". . . meanings are not in the message, they are in the message users."[2] If the speakers in negotiations do not adopt simple, direct, and mutually understood

---

[1] George A. Miller, *Language and Communications* (New York: McGraw-Hill Inc., 1951), p. 5.

[2] David K. Berlo, *The Process of Communications* (New York: Holt, Rinehart and Winston, Inc., 1960), p. 175.

language, they may end up "chasing themselves in verbal circles, unaware that they are making meaningless noises."[3]

The following terms are representative of those that should be understood among negotiators. The definitions are suggested; they should be modified when necessary so that both sides in the negotiating process will have common understanding.

American Federation of Teachers:

Union of classroom teachers affiliated with the American Federation of Labor and the Congress of Industrial Organizations. The National Union numbers about 150,000 members and has most of its strength in large bargaining units in large cities.

Arbitration (Arbitrator):

Method of settling employee-management dispute through recourse to an impartial third party whose decision is usually final and binding. Arbitration rulings in public employment are usually *advisory* (i.e., the impartial party recommends a settlement which is not binding). Arbitration is *voluntary* when both parties, of their own volition, agree to submit a disputed issue to arbitration, and *compulsory* if required by law.

Arbitrator:

Term used to designate impartial third party or member of a board to whom disputing parties submit their differences for decision (award).

Award:

In employee-management arbitration, the final decision of an arbitrator (binding on both parties to the dispute unless the situation calls for advisory arbitration in which case the award is a recommendation).

American Arbitration Association (AAA):

A private, nonprofit organization which supplies lists of arbitrators to parties. Most moderators in teacher negotiations come from

---

[3]Samuel I. Hayakawa, *Language in Action* (New York: Harcourt, Brace & World, Inc., 1940), p. 147.

"panels" sent out from AAA. AAA also conducts representation elections for determination of teacher negotiating units.

Bargaining:
See Collective Bargaining.

Board of Education (Board of Trustees) (School Committee):
The elected or appointed body of citizens charged with the responsibility of representing the public in policy development and supervision of management of a school district.

Checkoff:
Practice whereby the employer, by agreement with the employees' organization and upon written statement from each employee, regularly withholds organization dues from employees' pay and transmits these funds to the employee organization.

Collective Bargaining:
Method whereby representatives of the employees and employer determine the conditions of employment through direct negotiations, normally resulting in a written agreement or contract setting forth the wages, hours, and other conditions to be observed for the duration of the agreement. The phrase "collective bargaining" is used by the AFT in the teacher-negotiations arena.

Collective Negotiations:
This phrase is newly coined, combining part of the union phrase "collective bargaining" and the association phrase "professional negotiations."

Company Union:
Historically, a term used to describe a labor organization which is organized, financed, and/or dominated by the employer. Illegal under federal law since 1935.

Conciliation (Conciliator):
Attempt by a third party to help in the settlement of disputes between employers and employees through interpretation, suggestion, and advice (all of which is not binding). In practice, concili-

ation is synonymous with mediation. A conciliator is a person who undertakes conciliation of a dispute.

Contract:

A written agreement, generally of specified duration, arrived at as a result of negotiation between an employer and employees. The contract sets forth the conditions of employment (wages, hours, fringe benefits, etc.) and the procedure to be used in settling differences that may arise during the term of the contract (grievance procedure).

Demands:

Items proposed by the employees' organization for negotiation with the employer prior to a new contract (agreement) period, often referred to as proposals, offers, stipulations, or issues. The term is also used for items presented by the employer.

Dues:

The amount paid by employees to the employees' organization. Dues are used to support the program and activities of the organization. In the checkoff, the dues are withheld weekly or monthly.

Exclusive Representation:

Representation by one employee organization designated as the sole agent for negotiations with the employer.

Fact Finding:

Investigation of an employer-employee dispute by a board or panel, usually appointed by a chief executive of a government. Fact-finding boards issue reports which describe the issues in the dispute and frequently make recommendations for their solution.

Fringe Benefits:

General term used to describe supplemental benefits such as retirement plans, insurance, professional growth support, travel pay, disability pay, and sick leave received by employees in addition to regular salaries. Usually, the amount of compensation in addition to the regular salary is considered fringe benefits.

Good Faith:

A term used to describe the attitude and conduct of both parties in the negotiating process; both parties enter the negotiations with intent to reach an agreement that is generally satisfactory to both sides. This concept is difficult to define legally or to enforce; however, it implies that the parties honestly and sincerely attempt to reach an agreement.

Grievances:

Complaints or expressed dissatisfactions by an employee in connection with his work, salary, or other aspects of his employment. A complaint may be lodged for an alleged violation of law, agreement, or past practices. Usually, grievances are processed through a four-step operation which culminates in arbitration if there is no consensus.

Hours:

A term used to designate the time period of work during a day or week.

Impasse:

A deadlock in the negotiating process where there is no meeting of minds. Neither side will make further modification of its position. Usually indicated by a breakdown in the bargaining process where discussions cease and strikes or withdrawal of services occur.

Independent Union:

A union that is not affiliated with the American Federation of Labor and the Congress of Industrial Organizations.

Issue:

An item for negotiation proposed by the employee organization or the employer (*see* Demand).

Management:

Term applied to the employer and his representatives who are responsible for the administration and direction of an enterprise.

Managerial Prerogative:

The right or rights of management to maintain and operate the enterprise. Sometimes, these are spelled out by the contract; in other cases, management indicates that it has residual rights (i.e., all those not delegated away to the employee organization).

Mediation (Mediator):

A term used interchangeably with conciliation to mean an attempt by a third party to bring together the parties in a dispute. The mediator has no power to force a settlement (*see* Conciliation).

National Education Association:

An organization composed of educators from all segments of the education enterprise, including classroom teachers, specialists, and administrators.

Negotiation:

The process by which representatives of the employees and employers bargain to set conditions of employment including salaries, hours, benefits, working conditions, and the machinery for handling grievances.

Organization:

A term used to designate the binding together of a group of people to accomplish a goal or several goals. In the context of teacher-group action, the term is often used as an alternative to the terms "union" and "association."

Principal:

In education, the administrative head of a particular school.

Professional Negotiations:

A phrase used by the National Education Association as an alternative to the union term "collective bargaining." Refers to the process of negotiating or bargaining between employees and employers.

Representative:

Generally refers to an individual designated by the employees or the employer in collective negotiations. When used in connection with a group, reference is made to the negotiating representative.

Sanctions:

A technique for withholding services advocated by the National Education Association as an alternative to the strike advocated by unions. In applying sanctions, the state or national associations urge teachers not to seek employment in a particular school district or state as well as urging industries and businesses to avoid locating in the district or state. The purpose of the sanctions is to force the school district or state to improve conditions in education.

Settlement:

A successful conclusion to negotiations by common agreement of the parties involved.

Steward:

A union representative who carries out union duties among fellow workers; e.g., processing of grievances.

Strike:

A work stoppage by the employees in an enterprise for the purpose of gaining concessions from the employer.

Superintendent:

The chief administrative officer in a school district.

Supervisor:

A school employee who directs the work of others.

Teacher:

A school employee who spends all or part of time in the classroom and who is in direct contact with students in promoting the learning process.

Unit:

In the context of collective negotiations, the specific group organized for group action who are represented at the negotiating (bargaining) table; the combined group of employees who will be covered by a negotiating agreement.

Wages (salaries):

Employee compensation exclusive of fringe benefits.

Working Conditions:

The aspects of the employment environment exclusive of wages (salaries), hours, and fringe benefits.

Written Agreement:

The terms of a settlement that are reduced to writing and agreed to by both parties.

5

Questions and Answers

Many questions are raised when the parties to collective negotiations become involved in the process. In this chapter, the authors have selected some basic questions and proposed answers. The questions chosen do not exhaust the list of those that might be raised. However, they do illustrate problems and ideas with which negotiators must deal.

The Teacher Organizes

WHAT HAS CAUSED TEACHERS TO BECOME MORE MILITANT AND DISENCHANTED WITH THE TRADITIONAL SCHOOL BOARD-TEACHER RELATIONSHIPS?

Six major social and economic factors are generally attributed to teacher aggressiveness and the emergence of teacher militancy. Briefly described, they are:

1. the conflict inherent in the teacher's role as an "employee'" as distinguished from his professional role in the typically bureaucratic school system;

2. a rapid emergence of a new status for public employees in general, and the increasing pressures for enabling legislation at the state levels to provide organization and bargaining rights of which teachers can take advantage;
3. the increasing impatience of teachers with what they consider to be economic injustice. Teacher salaries have historically lagged behind the financial returns received by comparable trained groups, and often behind the pay of unskilled workers;
4. the pressures developing from the problems of large city school systems and the loss of identity by the teachers in large urban school systems.
5. the increasing educational level and professionalization of teachers which has activated the need for increased status and more dignity for the teaching profession;
6. the crusade of the American Negroes for human and civil rights—for elevation to first-class citizens. This has had a psychological effect on teachers, who have often considered themselves as the oppressed economic and social group. The activism of the civil rights movement and its effectiveness has significantly influenced the behavior patterns of teachers.

WHAT DOES "COLLECTIVE NEGOTIATIONS" MEAN?

The term "collective negotiations" refers to a set of procedures, usually in written form and officially adopted by the teachers' organization and the school board, which provides for an orderly method for reaching agreements about policies of mutual concern and for establishing channels for mediation in the event of an impasse.

In collective negotiations, the school board does more than just discuss issues with representatives from the teachers' organization. The school board is willing to engage in give-and-take sessions with teachers about policies of mutual concern. The school board and teacher representatives make proposals and counterproposals in good faith about the conditions of employment and other related matters with the objective of reaching mutually acceptable agreements.

WHAT ARE THE DIFFERENCES BETWEEN THE TERMS "PROFESSIONAL NEGOTIATIONS," "COLLECTIVE BARGAINING," AND "COLLECTIVE NEGOTIATIONS"?

The NEA advocates a series of procedures labeled professional negotiations while its rival organization, the AFT, advocates procedures called collective bargaining. Writers in the field of labor-management relations who do not want to show favor to either organization invented the compromise term "collective negotiations" to describe both procedures.

The actual differences between professional negotiations and collective bargaining are not completely clear. Many respected authorities have asserted that the differences between the two procedures are insignificant.

WHY DO TEACHERS WANT TO PARTICIPATE IN COLLECTIVE NEGOTIATIONS WITH THE SCHOOL BOARD?

In collective negotiations, the teachers as a group receive consideration and respect in the educational enterprise. Unilateral decisions (usually school-board policy) are replaced with a cooperative decision-making process. Each side presents arguments, facts, and reasons in favor of its own proposals. Whatever is mutually agreed upon becomes part of a contract under which the teachers and the administrators operate. When differences of interpretation or infractions of the agreement occur, grievance machinery provides for adjustments which may affect either or both sides in the dispute.

Teachers have definite contributions to make in a school system. They should be given the opportunity to participate in matters that concern their own welfare as well as to help resolve issues that affect educational policy. Collective negotiation arrangements allow this condition to become a reality.

IS COLLECTIVE NEGOTIATION INEVITABLE IN SCHOOL BOARD-TEACHER RELATIONS?

Since 1960, teachers have been seeking the right to negotiate with school boards regarding salaries, conditions of work, and other related matters. The movement is continually gaining momentum, which is demonstrated by the several hundred collective negotiation agreements that have already been adopted by local school districts. Both the National Education Association and American Federation of Teachers are committed to the philosophy that teachers' organizations should have the right to bargain collectively with school boards. Both organizations are staffed with highly trained and experienced specialists who are devoted to the objective of achieving the right of teachers to bargain collectively with school boards. Both organizations have the financial capability to implement and promote this objective. It is safe, then, to assume that the procedures of collective negotiations will spread to the fifty states and will have a significant impact in shaping the educational scene.

Teacher Organizations

DO TEACHERS HAVE THE LEGAL RIGHT TO JOIN EMPLOYEE ORGANIZATIONS?

In the past, this right has been questioned. Today, there is little doubt that teachers have the legal right to organize and join employee organizations. This includes professional associations as well as unions.

This legal right is founded upon the First and Fourteenth Amendments of the Constitution.

WHAT IS THE AMERICAN FEDERATION OF TEACHERS?

The American Federation of Teachers, first organized in 1916, is affiliated with the AFL-CIO. According to their official publication, the purposes and objectives of the AFT are very similar to those expressed by the NEA: to promote better schools, to obtain for teachers all rights to which they are entitled, to raise the standards of the teaching profession, and to promote the welfare of the children throughout the United States.

The AFT is specifically devoted to the promotion and advancement of classroom teachers. Superintendents, college presidents, and deans are prohibited from joining the AFT. The AFT does, however, allow each local organization to decide whether principals are eligible for membership.

The AFT is not structured on the basis of subject-matter departments, and the size and scope of AFT's national headquarters is limited compared to the NEA. It is estimated that the AFT has a membership of approximately 150,000 professional employees. Membership is concentrated mainly in large metropolitan areas.

WHAT IS THE NATIONAL EDUCATION ASSOCIATION?

According to official publications of the National Education Association, it is an independent, voluntary organization available to all professional educators. This organization believes that all educators, regardless of rank or job function, are workers in a common cause to improve education and to strive for better schools. To achieve this, the NEA is dedicated to the improvement of the professional status of teachers.

In 1967, the NEA had a membership of over one million. Approximately eighty-five percent of this membership consisted of classroom teachers.

The NEA is a very complex organization, consisting of approximately thirty-three departments and twenty-four commissions and committees, with seventeen headquarters. Their Washington headquarters employs a staff of over nine hundred persons, and the Research Division of the NEA is staffed with over twenty professional and administrative personnel assisted by about thirty-five office employees and statistical workers.

WHAT FACTORS MIGHT COMPEL TEACHERS TO JOIN THE AFT?

Some teachers feel that the AFT is more experienced, better prepared, and more structurally sound to exert economic pressure on boards of education and school administrators. Many teachers reason that an organization like the NEA, which allows conflicts of interests to penetrate its ranks, cannot serve teachers' needs in the negotiation process with school boards. These teachers believe that the NEA cannot represent them in terms of working conditions and welfare matters when administrators are included in the decision-making process of the teachers' organization.

Unless the NEA refuses membership privileges to school administrators, say this group of teachers, the AFT will continue to increase their membership until they become the dominant professional organization.

WHAT FACTORS MIGHT COMPEL TEACHERS TO JOIN THE NEA?

Some teachers feel that the NEA is a professional organization that can act independently of other organizations, while an organization like the AFT is linked with the labor movement and subservient to the parent organization, the AFL-CIO. These teachers believe that the NEA can negotiate effectively for welfare matters and working conditions while maintaining an independent and professional organization involving all professional personnel in the school system.

The severance of relationships with administrators leads to fragmentation and weakens the power of the AFT in the viewpoint of these teachers.

WHAT DOES THE TERM "PROFESSIONALISM" MEAN TO TEACHERS?

The term "professionalism" is used to connote the following characteristics of teachers:

1. a high degree of training in their teaching area, which includes knowledge of subject matter, the techniques and methods of teaching, and a sophisticated insight in the field of human growth and development;
2. a dedication and loyalty to their specialized area of knowledge, perhaps even more so than to the school district in which they are employed;
3. an unselfish devotion to the development of children;
4. an ability and willingness to participate in the decision-making process that affects not only their specialized teaching area, but the entire school system as well. Based upon their expertise and their dedication, administrative channels should be developed to encourage their participation.

Authority and Will to Negotiate

DO SCHOOL BOARDS HAVE THE LEGAL AUTHORITY TO NEGOTIATE WITH TEACHER ORGANIZATIONS?

It is commonly agreed that school boards possess the authority to negotiate with teacher organizations as well as the power to carry out agreements arrived at through collective negotiations. Furthermore, school boards can legally adopt negotiating procedures that guide their behavior, just as they can be guided by other rules and regulations.

It can be safely said that the courts will not interfere with reasonable regulations passed by school boards unless fraud, statute violation, or abuse of discretion can be demonstrated.

SHOULD THE SCHOOL BOARD AND SUPERINTENDENT RESIST THE ATTEMPTS OF A TEACHERS' ORGANIZATION TO NEGOTIATE WITH THE SCHOOL BOARD?

The demands for recognition and participation by teachers in the educational decision-making process have generally been categorized as teacher aggressiveness and teacher militancy. The impact of the initial demands of teachers for recognition and increased participation in policy-making decisions caught many school boards and superintendents off guard. Perhaps, in a great many cases, teachers and their organizations did not fully comprehend all the implications in the movement for increased participation.

As a result, school boards, superintendents, and teachers were a bit perplexed and concerned over the consequences of the movement. The first reactions of all parties were filled with doubt and suspicion. Extreme arguments of both sides seemed to gain major attention.

As school boards, superintendents, and teachers become more sophisticated at collective negotiations, they will form new attitudes and gain new perspective. School boards and superintendents will eventually feel that teachers should have a meaningful share in the formulation of educational policy decisions. First, personnel who have participated in the decision-making process will perform at higher levels of productivity, and second, if the proper channels of communications are open to them, teachers will contribute to the betterment of the educational program.

The Negotiators

WHO NEGOTIATES FOR TEACHERS?

The teachers' organization that enjoys the right of exclusive recognition is left free to determine the composition of its negotiating panel. The members of the negotiating panel are designated as the representatives of the teachers' organization that selected them. They are responsible to uphold the rules and regulations agreed upon by the membership of the teachers' organization.

It should be added that the negotiating panel is free to call in representatives from its state and national organizations to assist the local representatives promote their objectives to the school board.

WHO NEGOTIATES FOR THE SCHOOL BOARD?

The school board, like the teachers' organization, is free to determine the composition of its negotiating panel. It may designate the superintendent as the chief negotiator for the school board or the school board may appoint one of its own members to conduct the negotiation sessions.

Another possible avenue is to assign an outsider who is skillful in conducting collective negotiations the responsibility of negotiating for the school board. The school board may hire lawyers or other trained personnel to assist and to advise them during the negotiating sessions.

The Superintendent's Role

HOW DO THE MAJOR EDUCATIONAL ORGANIZATIONS VIEW THE SUPERINTENDENT'S ROLE IN COLLECTIVE NEGOTIATIONS?

The National Education Association (NEA) views the superintendent's role in collective negotiations as that of functioning in a dual capacity. He is, on the one hand, the executive officer of the school board, being responsible for administering adopted policies. On the other hand, the superintendent is the leader of the professional staff, having responsibilities to the teachers and their professional organization. In the negotiation process, the superintendent has the responsibility to both teachers and school-board members to help clarify issues, convey information to both sides, and assist both parties to achieve agreements which are in the best interest of the total school program.

The American Association of School Administrators (AASA) views the superintendent's role as one of an independent third party in the negotiating process. According to the AASA, the superintendent in the negotiating process should exercise free and independent judgments, reviewing each proposal in light of its effects upon the total school program. He should provide resource materials and information to both sides in an attempt to reach agreements based upon what is best for the educational program.

The National School Boards Association (NSBA) visualizes the superintendent's role as one of an administrative officer of the school board who interprets and channels teacher concerns to the board of education, and those responsibilities and concerns of the board of education to the teacher. If this proves inadequate, direct hearings with the school board can be arranged through the superintendent. Although the NSBA rejects the principle of teachers negotiating directly with the school board, it did reaffirm its long-standing position regarding the right of teachers to discuss with the school board details of salary, working conditions, and other matters pertinent to the welfare of the teachers.

The view of the American Federation of Teachers (AFT) of the role of the superintendent in the board-staff relationship differs markedly from that of the AASA or the NEA. The AFT stipulates that it is unrealistic to view the superintendent as an impartial agent representing both the school board and the professional staff. The school board is considered as management and the teachers as employees, while the superintendent is placed as the executive officer of the school board. Therefore, reasons the AFT, the superintendent is committed to represent the school board during all phases of school board-staff relationships.

WHAT IS THE EMERGING ROLE FOR THE SUPERINTENDENT IN COLLECTIVE NEGOTIATIONS?

From all indications, the superintendent is beginning to function more like the executive officer and chief school negotiator for the school board. There is an increasing tendency to have school boards delegate to the superintendent the responsibility of negotiating with the representatives from the teachers' organization.

In this emergent role, the superintendent is granted all the necessary powers to make unilateral decisions which the school board is expected to support. Naturally, the school board first establishes policy boundaries which the superintendent is committed to follow. But the exercise of options and the initiation of alternate measures within the policy boundaries are considered the responsibility of the superintendent, thus making him the school board's chief strategist in collective negotiations.

As outlined, the superintendent is assigned a role similar to that of a company executive in private industry. There are not too many valid reasons why superintendents cannot be trained to handle negotiations with organized groups of teachers as competently and as effectively as business executives handle negotiations with organized employee groups. Moreover, the superintendent is generally a former teacher who is familiar with educational goals and objectives and is more likely to understand the problems and language of teachers.

WHY SHOULD A SCHOOL BOARD DEPEND UPON THE SUPERINTENDENT FOR LEADERSHIP IN COLLECTIVE NEGOTIATIONS?

First, school-board members are not in a position to know enough about their school systems to be able to bargain effectively. Second, the collective bargaining process is a time-consuming operation, requiring full-time personnel and a great deal of study. Third, if the superintendent does not actively participate in collective negotiations, he will eventually be bypassed by both teachers and school-board members, making him less effective as an administrator. Fourth, one can assume that the representatives of the teachers' organization will be knowledgeable and well trained in the collective negotiation process. If this training and expertise is not matched by the school board in the form of a well-informed and experienced superintendent, the board will be no match for a teachers' organization.

DOES THE SUPERINTENDENT GET ASSISTANCE FROM HIS ADMINISTRATIVE STAFF WHEN HE IS CONDUCTING NEGOTIATIONS FOR THE SCHOOL BOARD?

Naturally, the superintendent does not enter into collective negotiations without assistance from his administrative staff. In almost all instances, the superintendent should draw upon the expertise of his building administrators and central office personnel. In large school systems, the personnel director might serve as the key advisor to the superintendent. The "superintendent's team" supplies him with needed information and plans strategies for future negotiation sessions. In addition, professional labor-relations experts from private industry may also assist the superintendent and his team in the collective negotiation proceedings.

The superintendent, with his negotiating team, focuses attention on known problems and new problems and their possible solutions. They are continually anticipating the likely proposals and counterproposals of the teachers' organization and the arguments that will be used against their own proposals. In this setting, they can match the trained and experienced negotiators that teachers' organizations will undoubtedly bring to the bargaining table.

The Administrator and Employee Organizations

SHOULD ADMINISTRATORS OF A SCHOOL DISTRICT BE REPRESENTED BY THE LOCAL TEACHERS' ORGANIZATION?

School administrators might strongly object to having a teacher-dominated organization negotiate for them. Teachers generally outnumber administrators and, therefore, can outvote them on almost all major policy matters. Another pertinent fact is whether school administrators can function in an effective manner when the persons they supervise are the same people who negotiate their conditions of work with the school board.

Another factor should also be considered. If school administrators are in the teachers' negotiating unit and still insist on negotiating on a separate basis for salaries, teachers might feel that the administrators made a deal to depress teachers' salaries while increasing their own salaries.

HOW ARE BUILDING PRINCIPALS BEING AFFECTED BY SYSTEM-WIDE COLLECTIVE NEGOTIATION AGREEMENTS?

Teachers are gaining and exercising the right to participate in determining rules and regulations which the principals are expected to administer. Generally, grievance procedures allow teachers to publicly bring complaints against principals who violate the intent of written agreements. In essence, teachers acting in concert are exercising the right to monitor and expose the administrative performance of principals, while the principals' right to monitor and expose the teachers' performance is declining. Yet, principals are still expected to administer the building in relation to the high level of responsibility and expectations established by the superintendent and board of education.

Principals, in order to protect themselves, have expressed a willingness to participate in determining the rules and regulations which they have to administer.

CAN TEACHERS EFFECTIVELY PROMOTE POLICIES THAT ARE IN DISAGREEMENT WITH THEIR ADMINISTRATION IF THE LOCAL TEACHERS' ORGANIZATION INCLUDES ADMINISTRATIVE PERSONNEL?

School administrators are very interested in teacher welfare and generally want teachers to receive satisfaction from their work. However, in the administrator's role of supervising teachers, there are bound to be conflicts of interest between teachers and administrators in determining conditions of work and about many aspects of the educational program. Is it then realistic to believe that teachers will be completely free and willing to express their opinions at their association meetings when local administrators are present?

One might say that administrators generally would never "take it out" on teachers who disagree; however, each teacher must decide if his administrator is an exception to this generalization. In short, it is quite possible that teachers may feel constrained by the presence of school administrators at teachers' organization meetings.

Negotiating Sessions

SHOULD THE ACTUAL NEGOTIATING SESSIONS BE CONDUCTED IN PRIVATE OR CLOSED MEETINGS?

People experienced in collective negotiations agree that the actual negotiating sessions should not be public meetings. In the "public eye," negotiators behave differently than they do in closed sessions. During public sessions, the parties in a dispute may be more prompted to uphold a position based upon political expediency. The school board may likely take a firmer stand and the teachers' organization may be more militant. When members of the press are present, they generally stress controversy rather than areas of agreement. In addition, policies may become more difficult to change once a public stand is taken.

In brief, informal give-and-take sessions as a basis for reaching agreements are more easily achieved in private sessions.

WHAT IS THE MEANING OF THE TERM "TO BARGAIN IN GOOD FAITH"?

Basically, bargaining in good faith implies a willingness on the part of each of the parties to listen to the views of the other, to take the other parties' viewpoint into consideration in reaching a decision, and to negotiate problems on which there are disagreements. Good faith implies "fairness" in assessing one's position with that advanced by the other party. Good faith is difficult to assign or judge quantitatively. It is a qualitative factor which demands adjudication and understanding from the parties.

Furthermore, bargaining in good faith requires that the parties involved be willing to meet at reasonable times and places and to allow a reasonable amount of time for discussion.

WHAT IS THE CAUCUS TECHNIQUE IN COLLECTIVE NEGOTIATIONS?

The caucus procedure in collective negotiations is utilized when one party in a dispute makes proposals not clearly acceptable or unacceptable by the other side. To study the short- and long-range implications of the proposals, the negotiating team holds private sessions to study the proposal and decide upon the best possible response.

WHAT ARE THE PROCEDURES IN COLLECTIVE NEGOTIATIONS WHEN THE SCHOOL BOARD IS NOT FISCALLY INDEPENDENT?

In this situation, the school boards are compelled to submit financial matters to municipal authorities for final approval. The negotiating sessions usually take place before the budget is submitted to the municipal agency. If the budget is reduced by the municipal agency, the budgetary allocations are then reduced according to a predetermined formula. If the budget is reduced beyond the expectations of the teachers, another round of negotiations usually takes place and the revised budget is again submitted to the municipal agency.

Another technique frequently used is to conduct three-party negotiations, including the school board, teacher organization, and the municipal agency. Or, informal communications with the municipal agency may be established while the school board and teachers carry on negotiations. In this manner, all concerned parties are continually informed as to the alternatives of the proposals.

WHAT ARE THE BENEFITS OF HAVING AGREEMENTS PLACED IN WRITING?

The purpose of collective negotiations is to have both parties reach an agreement. The process becomes more effective when the arrived-at agreements are placed in writing. In this manner, both parties have a copy of the rules, regulations, and rights that govern the relationship between the school board and teachers' organization. Although all controversy over the contents of the agreement is not eliminated, it is reduced considerably when both parties have a common document for reference. Also, writing helps clarify fuzzy thoughts and concepts and tends to reduce misunderstanding.

Negotiable Items

WHAT ARE THE MORE COMMON ISSUES CURRENTLY BEING NEGOTIATED BY SCHOOL BOARDS AND TEACHER ORGANIZATIONS?

A review of the research material pertaining to the contents of written agreements approved by school boards and teachers' organizations reveals that salaries, grievance procedures, sick-leave policies, and other conditions of work are the items most frequently mentioned. Items relating to professional matters including in-service programs, instruction, curriculum, and the health and safety of children are mentioned much less frequently.

The NEA has not yet reached its goal of negotiating with school boards all matters which affect the quality of the educational program, nor has the AFT reached its goal of negotiating any issue that affects the working conditions of teachers.

WHAT ARE SOME POTENTIAL AREAS OF CONFLICT BETWEEN SCHOOL BOARDS AND TEACHER ORGANIZATIONS?

One potential area of conflict is the teachers' demand for higher salaries and the expenditure of more funds for education in general.

A second area centers about rules and regulations that govern working conditions in the schools. Typically, these rules are established by school boards and administrators without teacher participation. Teachers are now demanding a sizable voice in the determination of these policies.

A third area of conflict relates to the concept of professionalism. Teachers more than ever feel that they are the experts in their specialized teaching areas and, therefore, should have a broad range of autonomy in determining how their teaching skills are utilized in the classroom.

MUST THE SCHOOL BOARD CONSIDER ALL ITEMS SUBMITTED BY THE TEACHERS' ORGANIZATION AS BEING NEGOTIABLE?

During the preliminary procedures of collective negotiations, the school board has to decide whether the items submitted by the teachers' organization are in the "realm" of negotiable items. The school board might decide that it hasn't the responsibility to negotiate a particular item; e.g., the construction of a vocational school for high school graduates. Second, the item may be considered non-negotiable based upon principles, rules, and regulations developed in school-board policies; e.g., the school board appoints all administrative personnel. Third, the item may be considered negotiable and within the authority of the school board, but action by another governmental agency is necessary before final approval can be given; e.g., a fiscally dependent school board submitting its budget to the city council. Lastly, the item may be considered a negotiable item.

There is no clear-cut way to distinguish negotiable from non-negotiable items. Almost all school-board decisions are elastic in that they affect the working conditions of teachers and the educational practices followed in the school system to some degree. Teachers may assert that such items as promotions, televised instruction, staff additions, curriculum content, school budgets, etc., relate to the conditions of work and to the educational program, and, therefore, are in the realm of negotiable items.

It is recommended that the school board should not compile a long list of non-negotiable items before the negotiation session begins. It may be wiser to allow teachers to discuss items that give them concern at the negotiating table. This does not mean that school boards should automatically relinquish the power of unilateral determination once the item is introduced by the teachers' organization. Instead, they should develop a rationale for the retention of unilateral control over matters that they feel deserve such treatment. This approach achieves the following desirable ends:

1. It alleviates contention resulting from a refusal on the part of the school board even to discuss matters on their own merit.
2. It requires school boards to justify by reason and knowledge their desire to maintain unilateral control over an item.
3. It exposes both parties to a different outlook, resulting in clearer understandings.

WHAT TOPICS ARE GENERALLY INCLUDED IN THE WRITTEN AGREEMENT?

The topics listed below are often included in a written agreement arrived at through collective negotiations:

a) recruitment of teachers
b) budget preparation
c) curriculum preparation
d) in-service training program
e) class size
f) salaries and fringe benefits
g) working conditions
h) teacher turnover
i) assignment
j) extra-curricular activities
k) tenure
l) daily schedule
m) merit pay
n) evaluation

Some school districts do not mention specific subjects, but remain flexible and comprehensive by including in the written agreement a statement that recognizes one organization and allows this organization to develop and present to the school board opinions on matters of concern to them.

Recognition

WHY DO TEACHER ORGANIZATIONS SEEK RECOGNITION RIGHTS?

The concept behind recognition is that the school board agrees to accept the teachers' organization as the authorized representative of the professional staff. This procedure is necessary if meaningful negotiations are to take place. Without recognition rights, each teacher has the burden of making his own arrangements with the school board. Naturally, teachers are virtually helpless to bargain effectively under this condition.

WHAT ARE THE POLICIES OF THE FOUR MAJOR EDUCATIONAL ORGANIZATIONS ON EXCLUSIVE RECOGNITION?

In 1965, the NEA adopted a policy of exclusive recognition by stating that the teacher's organizations that had majority support of the professional staff should be granted exclusive negotiation rights. Concurring with the NEA, the AFT stated that each local affiliation should seek exclusive negotiation rights through a democratic election involving classroom teachers.

In 1966, the American Association of School Administrators revised its no-policy position on exclusive recognition to one of favorable acceptance. The AASA's new policy advocates that all professional staff members should belong to a single organization which should be granted exclusive recognition rights.

The National School Boards Association, as late as 1965, expressed opposition to exclusive recognition and the collective negotiation process by stating that school boards should refrain from making compromise agreements based on collective negotiation procedures. In 1967, the NSBA recognized that teachers can "exercise full freedom of association, expression, organization and designation of representatives of their own choosing for the purpose of conferring with school boards concerning the terms and conditions of their employment."

HOW DOES A SCHOOL BOARD DETERMINE WHICH TEACHERS' ORGANIZATION SHOULD BE GRANTED RECOGNITION RIGHTS?

The selection of the teachers' organization to receive exclusive recognition rights is an easy one if there is only one teachers' organization in the school district. In such instances, the school board develops an exclusive recognition clause stating that the existing teachers' organization shall represent all certified employees of the school district for the purpose of participating in collective negotiations with the school board.

In school districts in which there are two teachers' organizations competing for recognition, the following patterns for selection usually emerge. The school board relates that it is willing to select the organization that has the largest membership of professional staff members. To determine this, the professional staff conducts a secret-ballot election to select the organization they want to represent them in the collective negotiation process with the school board. If a tight election is expected, the American Arbitration Association may be called in to establish voting procedures.

WHAT ARE THE MAJOR BENEFITS IN GRANTING EXCLUSIVE RECOGNITION?

Exclusive recognition compels teachers to resolve their disagreements concerning their objectives and tactics of collective negotiations before meeting with the school board. For example, certain segments of the teaching staff may desire substantial salary increases at the beginning levels of experience while another group of teachers may advocate the reduction of the number of steps to reach the maximum salary level. With exclusive recognition, these factions will have to rectify their differences among themselves before negotiations with the school board are scheduled to begin.

The second reason supporting the granting of exclusive recognition rights is a very practical and important one. Suppose the school board reaches an agreement with one teachers' organization and another teachers' organization insists on negotiating with the school board for a different agreement. The school board is then faced with an unsolvable dilemma because either teachers' organization can claim foul play against the school board if the agreement favors the other organization.

A third reason supporting exclusive recognition is that it allows for responsibility of action on the part of the school board and teachers' organization. The school board is required to meet with only a single organization and, therefore, is unable to evade its responsibility by citing disunity among the organization as a cause for inaction. Similarly, if the teachers are dissatisfied with the agreement, they can easily point out the responsible parties within their own organization. If their representatives do not adequately serve them, the teachers can affiliate with another organization or select new representatives.

HOW DOES EXCLUSIVE RECOGNITION DIFFER FROM FORMAL RECOGNITION?

Exclusive recognition means that the teachers' organization

enrolling a majority of the professional staff is given the right to enter into collective negotiations with the school board with the object of reaching an agreement applicable to all professional employees of the unit.

Formal recognition may be granted to the teachers' organization claiming the next largest membership (usually 10 per cent or more of the professional staff). Formal recognition status gives the teachers' organization the privilege of using the school facilities for meetings, being listed in the school directory, and having access to the school district's records. However, only the teachers' organization designated as the exclusive representative is entitled to enter into collective negotiations with the school board.

ARE THERE OTHER KINDS OF RECOGNITION?

To complete the list, two additional recognition plans must be mentioned:

1. Dual (joint) representation: This situation exists when the school board grants to two or more teacher organizations equal representation and equal rights to conduct collective negotiations with the school board. No distinctions are made on the basis of membership size or any other criterion. The representatives of the various organizations may meet separately or jointly with the school board to conduct collective negotiations.
2. Proportional representation: Under this plan, teacher organizations are represented on the collective negotiations committee on the basis of the proportion of teachers who are members of each local organization. Suppose organization X enrolls 600 teachers while organization Y enrolls 300 teachers. Then, organization X is entitled to twice as many representatives on the negotiating committee as organization Y.

HOW LONG SHOULD EXCLUSIVE RECOGNITION LAST?

The organization that wins exclusive recognition rights should be allowed a reasonable amount of time to carry out its policies before being challenged to a new election by a competing organization. The timing of the new representative election should be held prior to the school district's budgetary deadline, allowing the new teachers' organization reasonable opportunity to present its demands on the anticipated budget.

Many reliable sources suggest that representative elections be limited to once every two years. This would reduce the problem caused by budgetary deadlines, and would allow the school board and teachers' organization ample time to establish stable and meaningful relationships. This time span would not cause extreme hardships on teachers who are dissatisfied with their negotiating unit.

> DOES THE GRANTING OF EXCLUSIVE RECOGNITION PREVENT THE SCHOOL BOARD FROM COMMUNICATING WITH INDIVIDUALS OR MINORITY GROUPS?

There is nothing to prevent the school board from meeting with individuals or organizations representing classroom teachers for the purpose of hearing their views and opinions, except as they pertain to matters which are considered proper subjects for collective negotiations.

School boards, under exclusive recognition, still have the prerogative to hear a complaint of an individual employee against his supervisor or to have an individual process a grievance in his own behalf in accordance with the grievance procedure previously established.

Reaching an Impasse

> WHEN AN IMPASSE OCCURS, WHAT PROCEDURES MAY BE TAKEN TO AVOID A TEACHER STRIKE?

Obviously, outsiders in the form of a neutral third party must be brought into the dispute to act as catalysts or arbitrators. The various impasse procedures available are as follows:

1. Mediation: A neutral third party helps the negotiators settle a dispute through suggestion, advice, or other such stimulation. Mediation is a voluntary process, and the decision is not binding on either party.
2. Fact Finding: A third party conducts a formal hearing to investigate, assemble, and report the facts in a dispute. Each side in the dispute is given the opportunity to present its

case along with supporting evidence. Once the hearing has been completed, the fact-finder issues a public report, generally with recommendations. The theory behind this method is that the public will be inclined to accept the evidence and recommendations of the fact-finder, thus placing pressure on both parties to agree to the terms in the report.

3. Binding Arbitration: The parties submit their dispute to an impartial third party whose decision is final, requiring both parties to accept it. The preliminary method of investigating the dispute is similar to the formal hearing involved in fact finding.

4. Advisory (Non-Binding) Arbitration: This process is similar to binding arbitration, except that the decision is not final and binding. Advisory arbitration carries a strong recommendation to the parties in the dispute. The investigating procedures are similar to those used in fact finding.

Most states have an impasse procedure that involves their state department of education or their state labor relations board. Each of these agencies can provide skilled personnel in the field of employee-management relations. The selection of an appeal agency will generally depend upon state legislation that governs impasse procedures or on conditions stipulated in the local agreement between the school board and teachers' organization.

DOES THE SCHOOL BOARD GIVE AWAY A GOOD PORTION OF ITS POLICY-MAKING RESPONSIBILITIES WHEN IT ALLOWS MEDIATORS TO ASSIST IN SETTLING DISPUTES?

It should be pointed out that mediators have no authority to dictate a settlement to either party. Their role is strictly an advisory one. They only assist the parties in reaching agreements. Generally, mediators meet with both parties on a separate basis to determine what concessions each party will make to reach an agreement.

On the strength of such confidential information, the mediators are in a favorable position to propose a settlement that both parties may be willing to accept.

Again, mediation is a voluntary process; the final decisions and legal responsibilities still remain with the school board.

DO TEACHERS HAVE A LEGAL RIGHT TO STRIKE?

Traditionally, the courts have viewed teacher strikes as illegal acts. No state has granted teachers the right to strike. Statutes in several states prohibit public employees from striking and some state laws are more definite, mentioning teachers specifically.

WHAT ARE THE DIFFERENT TYPES OF SANCTIONS?

Sanctions may take different forms such as:

1. warning teachers not to apply for positions in a local school system or in a state school system;
2. advising the citizens of locality or state about adverse conditions in the school system;
3. advising that business and industry not plan to locate in locality or state because of poor school conditions;
4. censuring a school system for particular or general deficiencies;
5. A combination of any or all of the methods listed above.

WHAT ARE THE DIFFERENCES BETWEEN STRIKES AND SANCTIONS?

Both techniques attempt to exert persuasion against the public authorities for the purpose of gaining concessions for teachers. In the strike, there is an actual work stoppage. Sanctions do not involve an actual work stoppage but serve as a warning that, unless conditions improve, the school system may be adversely affected in the future.

ARE THE PROFESSIONAL ETHICS OF TEACHERS LIKELY TO PREVENT THEM FROM STRIKING?

One can safely conclude from an analysis of current teacher behavior that teacher professionalism not only permits but obligates teachers to withdraw their services when certain conditions exist in their school system. When the school district jeopardizes the welfare, safety, and educational program of the students, teachers often feel obligated to withdraw their services. This rationale is supported by the conduct of other professional groups. For example, doctors are not supposed to practice medicine under conditions that might endanger the welfare of patients. Lawyers are supposed to withdraw counsel when a client is determined to use unethical means to secure a favorable court ruling. An airline pilot will not take his plane off the ground when he feels the airplane is not safe. A priest will not offer a person salvation when certain conditions set down by the church have not been met.

Increasingly, teachers are following the professional conduct practiced by other professions of withdrawing services when conditions of employment are not satisfactory according to their professional judgment.

Grievance Procedures

WHAT ARE THE BASIC ELEMENTS OF A GRIEVANCE PROCEDURE?

A grievance procedure usually consists of a series of predetermined steps of appeal which a teacher can follow in order to rectify an alleged violation of a negotiated agreement. The first step is generally for the teacher to present the grievance to his immediate supervisor who is usually the building principal.

If satisfaction is not obtained at this level, he takes the grievance to the next appeal step. Generally, this step involves central office personnel, usually the personnel director or assistant superintendent.

If, in the eyes of the teacher, satisfaction is still not obtained, he presents the grievance to the person who represents the third step in the appeal procedure, usually the superintendent or board of education.

At this point, if satisfaction is still not achieved, the teacher generally has the right to obtain the opinion or ruling of a neutral third party. Generally, the third party is a mediation panel consisting of one member selected by the teachers' organization, one member selected by the school board, and a third member selected by these two people. Various agencies such as the American Arbitration Association and the Federal Mediation and Conciliation Service compile lists of impartial persons who are qualified to serve on mediation panels.

WHAT ARE THE OBJECTIVES OF A GRIEVANCE PROCEDURE?

A grievance procedure allows teachers to register complaints against the administration regarding an alleged incident that took place during school hours or about unsatisfactory conditions of work.

The primary purpose of a grievance procedure is to guarantee that all teacher complaints are handled through proper administrative and supervisory channels. Generally, formal grievance procedures are formulated so that either the principal or immediate supervisor is involved in the initial step in this process. This prevents teachers from bypassing building principals or line supervisors. If teachers are able to issue complaints directly to the superintendent, the principal is then placed in an ineffectual position. He is prevented from reacting to and resolving the complaint of the grieved teacher.

Some Other Questions

WHAT KIND OF INFORMATION DO SCHOOL BOARDS AND ADMINISTRATORS NEED TO PREPARE FOR COLLECTIVE NEGOTIATIONS?

Effective negotiations and the attainment of objectives require more than the casual presentation of proposals, instinctive responses, or the "playing it by ear" technique. Careful preparation must include the selection and development of proposals and facts based upon valid research.

Facts for collective negotiations should include the following information:

1. What is the general economic structure of the national, state, and local school district? This area of information may include data about tax rates, millage levies, federal and state aid, and the anticipated costs to implement the educational plans of the school district. School boards should have facts on policies, salaries, fringe benefits, and cost comparisons from comparable school districts.

2. Based upon the opinions and viewpoints of the central office staff and building principals, information regarding unsolved problems and anticipated problems within each school building should be identified.

3. The administrative staff should be consulted to establish

priorities of needs, and to prepare strategies for proposals and counterproposals. With this information, the school board should establish priorities of objectives, including the changes in policies and practices that the school board desires. Fall-back positions should be agreed upon so that the school board can "bargain off" lesser objectives for more significant ones.

4. The school board and administrative staff should be constantly anticipating teacher proposals and the possible arguments teachers might use against proposals submitted by the school board.

WHICH AGENCY SHOULD REGULATE THE COLLECTIVE NEGOTIATION PROCESS IN EDUCATION?

Because the NEA and AFT have conflicting opinions, the issue is usually discussed in terms of "educational channels" versus "labor channels."

The NEA strongly believes that such education-oriented agencies as the state departments of education, colleges, and universities should establish operational guidelines for impasse procedures and precedents that would regulate and guide collective negotiations in education.

In opposition to this viewpoint, the AFT continually reaffirms that state labor-relation agencies which operate on the basis of state labor laws and regulations should regulate and guide the collective negotiation process, in the belief that labor-oriented rules and regulations that have been proven satisfactory in solving disputes in the private sector of the economy will also prove satisfactory in the educational sector.

When an impasse occurs, the AFT favors the utilization of mediators and conciliators affiliated with the state labor-relation agencies rather than personnel attached to educational organizations. Alternatives to labor or educational channels are such organizations as The American Arbitration Association and The New York State Public Employee Relations Board.

WHAT KINDS OF LEGISLATION ARE TEACHERS REQUESTING IN COLLECTIVE NEGOTIATIONS?

Teachers are seeking legislation that will guarantee them the right to join an organization and the right to exclusive recognition.

In addition, they are seeking legislation regarding the following procedures in collective negotiations:

1. designating a unit of representation;
2. defining the scope of negotiations;
3. specifying written agreements;
4. specifying educational systems to be involved;
5. good-faith negotiating;
6. listing of prohibited practices;
7. prohibiting strikes;
8. setting up impasse procedures;
9. designating an impartial agency to administer the law;
10. specifying the length of agreements.

WHAT IS A DUES CHECK-OFF PROCEDURE?

To obtain financial security for their teachers' organization, teacher organization officials often request that the central administrative office deduct organization dues from payroll checks and deposit the money into the bank account belonging to the teachers' organization. Each teacher must authorize such deductions before the school administration will comply with the request.

There are several reasons teacher organizations request this procedure. First, the expense of collecting membership dues is transferred to the administrative offices. Second, collecting dues directly from each teacher is often a difficult task. Third, it avoids the problem of having to collect back dues from teachers in good standing in the organization. Often, this situation proves embarrassing to the membership ranks, especially when back dues accumulate to a large amount of money.

6

Hypothetical Case Study: Organization and Collective Negotiations in Public Education

Glenco, West Nebasota, is a moderately sized city with a school system consisting of twelve elementary schools, two junior highs, and two senior high schools. Glenco citizens take considerable pride in their educational system and defend it accordingly; yet these citizens, for the most part, are unaware of the discontent lingering beneath the visual surface of the system itself.

The Glenco Board of Education, consisting of seven responsible and unpaid members of the community, has the responsibility of determining the teachers' salary schedule, allocating funds for educational costs, and together with the superintendent of schools, determining general classroom and non-classroom policies. The policies are interpreted and applied as rules and procedures by each school's principal to be obeyed and followed by each teacher. The majority of enforcement is one of "rigid observance of board policy and applied procedures."

The faculty of Glenco schools, numbering 330 professional staff members, has, in the past, been a dissatisfied, yet passive lot. One source of complaint has been the pay structure. The base salary for beginning teachers is slightly less than the average for schools in surrounding districts, and the rate of progression for more experienced teachers is considerably less. However, the greatest elements of discontent seem to stem from non-monetary issues. The teachers value themselves as professionals and are sincerely desirous of providing the children of Glenco with a profitable education. But they are dissatisfied with having little voice in the establishment of classroom procedures and with being allowed little individual initiative and discretion in teaching methods. In addition, they consider themselves overburdened with many non-teaching tasks such as hall duties, lunchroom duties, recess duties, and the updating and completion of numerous detailed reports.

An indicator of this dissatisfaction is the relatively high rate of teacher turnover. The faculty has rarely taken action to correct the conditions except, perhaps, to speak separately with the principals. Occasionally, a grievance reaches the school board, but if satisfaction is not granted, no further action is instigated. The result has been that teachers who were mobile soon left for other jobs, and the teachers who were firmly rooted in the community resigned themselves to the inevitable.

Organization by state affiliates of the National Education Association and the American Federation of Teachers was attempted several times in the past, but with no substantial success. Various reasons are cited for these failures; some teachers thought it unprofessional to be associated with a labor union, others thought they would be looked upon with contempt by the citizens of the community, and still others thought that it would simply be to no avail to organize. The consensus, however, is that the primary reason for the failures was the attitude of the school administrators. Considerable difficulty in organizing the teachers was caused by public statements of administrators expressing hostility toward having teachers participate in collective negotiations and giving teachers a voice in the decision-making process. Although a small number of teachers were members of the NEA and the AFT, there seemed to be, at least until October of 1966, little possibility of a union or association to overcome obstacles to actively represent the teachers of the Glenco school system. At an informal meeting of officers of the AFT and NEA, a decision was reached to call a system-wide meeting of all non-administrative professional staff members.

Organization of Teachers

On October 10, the special meeting of the entire faculty from all sixteen schools was conducted by the leadership of the AFT and NEA organizations. The stated purpose of this meeting was a discussion among teachers, counselors, psychologists, and nurses (but excluding all administrators) concerning possible methods for eliminating the sources of discontent—in short, organization.

Since attendance at this meeting was far greater than at the regular organization meetings, this may have been an indication that the attitude of caution toward organization had diminished. Also present were state representatives of the NEA and AFT who wanted to present a positive picture of collective negotiations among the profession and to initiate the beginning procedures toward organization.

For nearly an hour, the state representatives of the NEA and AFT listened to the faculty discuss the pros and cons of organization. Finally, one of the representatives posed a simple question to the group: "In what ways other than organizing your efforts for concerted activity can you bring about any improvement in the conditions which exist in the Glenco school system?" No one in the group, at least orally, could make any such suggestion. By a voice vote, the faculty group agreed that the officers of the local NEA and AFT should establish procedures necessary for gaining negotiation rights with the school board.

The officers of the teacher groups contacted the superintendent to request a meeting with him and the school board to discuss several significant steps necessary for establishing collective negotiations as well as to develop communications with the central office personnel and the school board. The superintendent arranged a meeting for October 17 at 4:30 P.M. for the school board and the officials of the teacher groups.

The first meeting between the school board, superintendent, and teacher representatives was a friendly, but cautious one. Neither side knew what to expect from the other. The atmosphere of the meeting continually improved when the board members began realizing that the teacher groups did not come to "air out their gripes," but were sincere and reasonable about wanting to improve their conditions of work.

Several important decisions were reached at this meeting. First, that an election would be conducted to establish whether organization was desired. Second, that the teachers would vote on which teacher organization was to represent them. Finally, both groups agreed that the American Arbitration Association should be contacted for the purpose of conducting the election and determining the negotiating unit.

As a result of this meeting, the school board sent a letter to each teacher in Glenco stating its belief that teachers should be given the opportunity of voting to determine whether they wished to present their problems to the school board through an organization of their own choosing. The letter also indicated that in the very near future teachers would have the opportunity to determine which teacher organization was to be their representative and that the teachers would determine who should be represented by the negotiating unit. The letter concluded by stating that the superintendent was instructed to contact the American Arbitration Association to request assistance in carrying out these policies.

Planning for Teacher Recognition

A field team from the American Arbitration Association met with the superintendent and officials of the NEA and AFT to finalize the procedures for the election that would allow teachers to decide which organization would represent them in negotiations with the school board.

The date of the election was set for November 28, 1966, thus allowing adequate time for campaigning and for the voters to become well informed about the various alternatives. It was decided that the location of the polling place would be in the junior high school and it would be staffed by an impartial citizens' organization, the Glenco League of Women Voters. Voting would be by secret ballot, and each ballot would include the sole question, "Do you desire to be represented by the Glenco Education Association, the Glenco Federation of Teachers, or no organization?"

Before the planning of the election procedures could continue, the arbitration team had to render a decision on the eligibility to vote of certain groups of employees, thus determining the composition of the negotiating unit. The AFT officials proposed that only those persons who were certified personnel and employed on the basis of the classroom teachers' salary schedule could be part of the negotiating unit. The officials of the NEA objected to these membership limitations and advocated a negotiating unit that included all members of the certified staff, including principals, assistant principals, department heads, librarians, guidance counselors, and all other non-teaching personnel.

After lengthy discussions with the teacher-organization officials, the arbitration team ruled that principals and assistant principals should be excluded from the negotiating unit, but that department heads, librarians, speech therapists, guidance counselors, nurses, and social workers should be included. Their decision was based primarily on the extent to which this group of employees shared common functions, skills, educational attainment, wages, managerial supervision and other characteristics that gave them a "community of interests."

Based upon the ruling of the arbitration team, the Board of Education supplied a complete list of eligible voters to the AAA, the two competing organizations, and to the school administration. One member from each of the three groups, the NEA, the AFT, and the administration, was permitted as an observer at the polling places for purposes of witnessing the election, certifying the count, and if they desired, challenging the eligibility of voters.

Campaigning prior to the election was extensive but well within the limitations recommended by the AAA. Conduct of all promotional activity was held to a high standard since it was recognized by the faculty that this election actually involved not only the teachers, but the pupils, their parents, and the community as a whole. No evidence of the upcoming election was existent in the classroom and the normal operation of the school system was not disrupted. Organizers for the two organizations were allowed to solicit for support only during times of non-academic scheduling. However, it was realized by supporters of both organizations that the same prejudices and fears of administrative reprisal that had been prevalent in the past would have to be overcome before November 28, so the campaigning outside of the classroom and during non-teaching hours was vigorous.

The urgency of the teachers' problem, the campaigning, and the intense feelings for and against organization seemed to induce a high rate of voter turnout. Tabulation of the voting revealed that 295 of the 306 eligible voters had cast ballots. The results of the voting were as follows:

Voter Choices	Number of Votes
Glenco Education Association—NEA	140
Glenco Federation of Teachers—AFT	129
No Organization	26

Faculty preference for organization was dominant by a vote of approximately eight to one. However, preference for NEA affiliation was only slightly greater than that for AFT representation.

Since the results of the election indicated a strong desire for organization but with no strong organization preference, and because the state law of West Nebasota did not require exclusive recognition of one teachers' organization, the American Arbitration Association provided the Glenco faculty with two certification alternatives. First, the teachers could decide to be represented exclusively by either the NEA or AFT, depending on which received the most votes in a second election. The ballot for this election would include only those two choices, excluding the choice of "no organization." Second, the teachers could decide to maintain a system of joint-negotiation in which both organizations would be represented on the teachers' negotiating team.

Open rivalry between the two teacher organizations increased. Each organization wanted to gain exclusive recognition rights with the school board. But the NEA and AFT were uncertain about their strength and wanted to avoid an open confrontation at this time. Since this was the teachers' first attempt at collective negotiations, the faculty had not yet formed a system of rigid alliances. The American Arbitration field team instructed the officials of each organization to poll their membership to determine which type of recognition was desired. Both organizations agreed to accept the joint-negotiation proposal.

To guard against operational failure, the American Arbitration field team established guidelines for the composition of the joint-negotiation committee. It was decided that the committee would consist of seven people selected by the teacher organizations on a proportionate basis determined by membership. Each teacher organization would adopt provisions for selecting its proportionate share of members to the joint-negotiation committee. The members of the joint-negotiation committee would then select a chairman from its own membership. The NEA and AFT representatives would be required to coordinate their negotiating in such a way as to present a unified set of issues and negotiate one agreement with the school board.

The school board, on December 12, 1966, granted recognition to the joint-negotiation unit which represented the two organizations that enrolled the majority of teachers in the Glenco school system.

Preparation for the First Negotiations: The School Board

Mr. Butler, Superintendent of Schools, began to "ready" his school board and administrators for the process of negotiating with representatives of the teacher organizations. He initiated a series of meetings with the school board and administrative staffs to establish a negotiating team and to formulate plans for negotiations. It was decided that Mr. Butler would act as the chief negotiator for the school board; he deemed it essential that the other team members include: (1) a representative from each school level, so that questions raised by the teacher negotiators could be adequately handled; (2) representatives occupying positions high enough on the hierarchy to lend dignity and status to the negotiating procedures; (3) representatives respected by their colleagues and able to communicate to their respective school levels a sense of wide participation in framing the final agreement, so that the administration of the agreement would be in the hands of administrators who would feel that they had played an effective part in writing the terms of the contract. On the basis of those standards, the school board's negotiating team included the following members: one board member, one principal from the elementary schools, one principal from the secondary schools, the personnel director, and business manager. Mr. Butler would act as the chairman and chief negotiator of the school board's negotiating committee.

It was further stipulated that all proposals agreed upon by the school board's negotiating committee would have to be approved by a majority of the board before the agreement could become a legal document.

Mr. Butler held several preliminary meetings with the school board's negotiating team to discuss some techniques of negotiations. He advised the members that they should remain calm even when placed in difficult circumstances or confronted with issues dissonant with their own value system. He cautioned that the first negotiating meeting, and indeed several thereafter, might be charged with emotionalism and heated issues. He also pointed out that the state representatives of the NEA and AFT who would be advising the local representatives were experienced, hard-nosed, and clever negotiators. Mr. Butler advised the group that the teacher negotiators might attempt some "blue-sky bargaining" to eventually get more than they could rightfully expect by taking less than they had originally asked.

The school board's negotiating team established several measures of evaluation to assist them in determining the consequences of the demands proposed by the teacher negotiating team.

Cost

1. Short-range cost—for the next school year and the amount of immediate funds needed.
2. Long-range cost—once the demands are implemented, the built-in cost increases that will occur as teachers move up the salary schedule or add to their teaching experience.
3. Cost of administration—the amount of extra administrative personnel, supervision, and equipment that will be needed to implement the demand.
4. Alternate plan—other methods of achieving objectives of demands without increasing costs: tying proposals into existing system, rearranging structure of school organization, reassigning personnel, etc.

Value

1. To teachers—as a morale factor, quality of teaching, hiring and retention of teachers, retirement plan.
2. Value to students—increased learning experiences in the classroom, better methods of instruction, more suitable environment for teaching and learning.
3. Value to school system—improving caliber of instruction, upgrading teacher expertise, attaining a higher level of preparation of teaching staff.

The superintendent, the school board, and administrators formulated plans for achieving the following objectives: (1) introduction of in-service training programs before school opened, (2) implantation of the idea of merit pay into the thinking of the faculty, (3) initiation at a future date of increased supervision of classroom instruction. Naturally, the school board did not expect their negotiating team to gain all these objectives, but they felt confident that teachers would accept at least one of their proposals. And the seeds of thought would have been planted for future negotiating sessions.

The school board outlined for their negotiating team the maximum salary increases that they would be willing to offer the teachers. The team would have to function within these boundaries.

By evaluating each proposal in relation to its merit—for teachers, students, and the school system—and to its cost and implementation, the negotiating team of the school board could establish a priority of objectives in working toward desirable results in negotiations.

Preparation for the First Negotiations: The Teachers

The officers of the NEA and AFT held separate meetings with their membership to discuss the kinds of proposals that would be submitted to the school board. Present at each meeting were representatives of their respective state organizations. The discussions were lively, the proposals centering about three topics: salaries, conditions of work, and the educational program. Some of the suggestions made by the faculty were nothing more than personal gripes, but a great many made "educational sense" and displayed a thorough knowledge of the problems that existed in the school system. Using the thinking of their membership, the officers of each organization with their state representatives drafted a list of proposals that reflected the most important concerns of the faculty.

Since two separate sets of issues could not be presented to the school board, it was up to the officers of the NEA and AFT with their state representatives to coordinate the proposals of each organization into one set of issues. Since the sources of discontent were common to both groups, this coordination was not difficult to achieve. Each group compiled a list of five issues; four of these issues were virtually identical and the fifth of each group differed.

The following comprise the four issues which both the NEA and the AFT groups agreed should be pursued:

1. the increase of the base salary for beginning teachers by $600 per year, and the increase of each succeeding increment from the present $200 to $300 between steps on the salary schedule;
2. the hiring of teacher aides (one for every three classroom teachers) to relieve the teachers of non-instructional duties, such as recess and lunch-room supervision and the general clerical duties required of the faculty;

3. the establishment of a district-wide teacher committee for the approval of textbooks and other materials of instruction;
4. the establishment of a grievance procedure.

In addition to the above proposals, the NEA committee suggested that:

- a maximum classroom ratio of one teacher to thirty students be established. Any class in excess of thirty students would require one additional full- or part-time teacher.

The fifth proposal of the AFT committee suggested that:

- teachers have three days of absence with pay for personal reasons other than for illness per school year (personal leave days).

Each committee decided to include in their list of proposals the fifth demand of the other group. Thus, the coordinated efforts of NEA and AFT produced six issues.

The next procedural step was to present the proposals for negotiation to the faculty and gain their approval. Copies of the six issues were given to every teacher at special faculty meetings called by the two teacher organizations. Almost 100 per cent of the membership of each group voted to support the proposals. It was further agreed that the membership in the negotiating unit would have the opportunity to vote to accept or reject the agreement arrived at through collective negotiations.

To obtain the strongest negotiating team and still abide by the seven-man limitation, the teacher groups selected the following representatives: two officers from the local AFT, three officers from the local NEA, one state representative of the AFT, and one state representative of the NEA. The teachers' negotiation team selected Mr. Williams, Vice-President of the local NEA, as their chief negotiator. The joint-negotiating committee believed that he was emotionally suited for the position and sufficiently aware of the problems of the school system. He was also respected and well thought of by the teachers and school board.

Having received authorization from the faculty, the joint-negotiation committee proceeded to the office of the Glenco Board of Education to present the list of issues. The secretary of the board received the committee, accepted their memorandum, and told them they would be notified concerning the impending course of action following the next board meeting.

Hypothetical Case Study

The teachers' joint negotiating team began to prepare for the future negotiation sessions. Being completely inexperienced in the negotiating procedure, the teachers on the negotiating committee were forced to rely heavily upon the AFT and NEA state representatives. The state representatives were quick to inform the joint-negotiation committee that thorough and painstaking preparations were needed prior to the first session—greater preparations than merely forming a list of issues—so that they would not find themselves at a decided disadvantage which might force them to make unnecessary concessions or lead the negotiations into serious impasses. With this in mind, the committee began the task of preparing data. Economic information pertaining to salary schedules of surrounding communities, cost-of-living indexes, and other economic factors was gathered. Information about fringe benefits and policies regulating teacher-pupil ratio was gathered from comparable school districts. Charts and graphs were developed to implement the demands. Expected costs of each of the demands were computed. To counter an argument of inability to pay, the committee reviewed the educational costs and funds structure. Fall-back positions were agreed upon to allow them to "bargain off" lesser objectives for more significant ones.

Getting to the Negotiating Table

The organized movement of the Glenco teachers had been going smoothly and seemed to be picking up momentum. When the reply from the school board was finally received, it seemed that all that had been hoped for might be threatened. The school board replied that it could not accept the proposals. A partial statement of the reply was as follows:

> We have received your memorandum of proposals and have carefully considered them. We are not managers of private enterprise. We do not seek profits, we are unpaid, and we do not fear for our jobs.
> Our duty is to provide the best possible education for the children of Glenco with the least possible cost to the citizens. Because of the nature of your list of issues, we cannot accept your proposals.
> We would suggest the following proposals:
> 1. Change the base salary for beginning teachers by $200 and increase the increment to $225.
> 2. Employ five teacher aides for the entire system.

3. Continue the textbook selection system presently employed.
4. Establish a grievance procedure.
5. Maintain the present practice of classroom pupil-teacher ratio.
6. Continue the present leave system.
7. Introduce an in-service training program before school opens.
8. Appoint a committee to study a professional merit system.
9. Begin to plan for increased supervision of classroom instruction.

The Board of Education hopes that the teachers will accept these proposals and thus preclude the necessity for a negotiating meeting.

Immediately upon receipt of the board's reply, the officers of the NEA, AFT, and the negotiation committee met to discuss various alternatives. Acting as advisors in this discussion were the state representatives of the NEA and AFT. The teacher organizations felt the school board was attempting to test the strength and determination of the teachers.

Wasting no time, the chief negotiator of the joint-negotiation committee requested a meeting with the school board. He began by informing the board that the joint-negotiation committee should not be considered an outside force, but rather the speaking representative of the entire Glenco faculty. It was further stated that the presentation of the six issues by the committee was not an attempt at selfish gains nor was it done with any intention of harming the educational system. Rather, it was done with a desire to make the Glenco school system stronger by improving the status of the teachers, by improving the competitive positions for new teachers, by improving teacher morale, and by allowing the teachers to concentrate upon instructional duties. The chief negotiator for the teacher group then instructed the school board that if it did not intend to negotiate by February, the following sanctions would be instigated:

1. Every faculty member of the Glenco schools would be urged to take an "illness" absence until the school board agreed to negotiate in good faith with the joint-negotiation committee.
2. Public censure would be solicited through mass media and professional publications.

3. Members presently employed would be advised that, if arrangements permitted, they should seek employment elsewhere.
4. Advertisements would be placed in the employment sections of surrounding newspapers indicating the low salary and poor working conditions to which Glenco teachers were subjected.

Since there was every indication that the majority of teachers actually were going to feign sickness and that the teacher organizations really would apply the sanctions, the school board soon indicated its willingness to meet with the joint-negotiation committee to discuss the issues. A date of February 6 was set by the parties for the first meeting in the negotiation process.

The Negotiation Process

The superintendent and the chief negotiator of the joint-negotiation committee met several days prior to the starting date of the negotiations in order to establish the ground rules for the negotiating sessions. The rules established at this meeting were: (1) Each meeting would last no longer than four hours per session unless both parties wished to continue. (2) The size of the negotiating committees present at each session would be no larger than seven members. (3) Specialists could be called by either party as long as each committee did not exceed ten members. (4) Proposals and counterproposals could be offered by either party at any time during the negotiation. (5) If a contract settlement agreeable to both parties could not be reached by April 1, 1967, it would be considered an impasse in the negotiating process and sanctions could be used. No forms of sanctions could be used before April 1. (6) The negotiating meetings would be private and limited only to team members.

During the first session, little negotiating occurred. The negotiators devoted the first several hours to acquainting themselves with the negotiation procedures to be followed.

Dialogue—Second Session: Priority of Demands

BUTLER (B): We looked over your list of demands and according to our figures, it would cost the school district over $250,000 on just salary increases.

That means a large jump in the tax rate, which is already too high.

WILLIAMS (T): Yes, we understand this, but we also did some checking. The Glenco School District has the lowest tax rate when compared to similar-sized school districts in the state. It can well afford additional outlays for good teachers.

BUTLER (B): The cost-of-living index doesn't justify such a sharp increase in salaries.

WILLIAMS (T): That depends on whose price index you're looking at. Our average salary level is well below the average for the state and we're better trained, too.

BUTLER (B): I am sure that the school board would look more favorably at granting salary increases to teachers if they knew they were putting more effort into their teaching.

WILLIAMS (T): Our teachers do a lot more work than the teachers in many school districts around Glenco. We surveyed the Glenco High School staff to determine how much time they spend on extra-curricular activities. Would you believe four hours per week per faculty member?

BUTLER (B): Well, that may be true. Many of the faculty members are dedicated and do a wonderful job with the boys and girls. But I'm talking about the minority who just don't give a damn anymore.

WILLIAMS (T): We don't have too many of that kind at Glenco.

BUTLER (B): That's the point. We do have some. Should the taxpayers reward incompetent teachers? Naturally not!

WILLIAMS (T): Are you injecting the question of merit pay?

BUTLER (B): Yes. I just don't like the idea of rewarding incompetent teachers with salary increases.

WILLIAMS (T): That's not reason enough to keep all salaries below the average in the state. The teachers want and deserve across-the-board salary increases. This is quite necessary if Glenco wants to continue to attract and retain well-qualified teachers. I think that parents realize this and do support the faculty. Look how many merit scholarships the Glenco students have won.

BUTLER (B): I'm aware of the merit scholarship record. But that doesn't detract from my point. What I would like to do is to organize a committee to study the in-service program of the Glenco faculty for possible upgrading of instruction. What I mean is this: an in-service training program that would begin one week before school begins and be devoted to instructional improvement.

WILLIAMS (T): That sounds like a worthwhile idea. Of course the faculty would participate in the planning of the in-service program. But let me ask you this question: Would the teachers be paid for their extra week of work?

BUTLER (B): Well, no, but that's a good way to justify your salary increases to the community.

WILLIAMS (T): What you're saying is that we shouldn't receive real salary increases but just get paid extra for overtime work.

BUTLER (B): If you agree to the in-service training program, perhaps we could talk about a salary adjustment for the in-service program.

WILLIAMS (T): That's fine with me. I am anxious to see concrete figures on this. My colleagues on the negotiation team would want time to study your specific proposal once it is submitted.

The Sixth Session: Further Progress

Several additional meetings were held. Dialogue between the two parties continued. At the sixth meeting, the superintendent informed the joint-negotiation team that the school board had again reviewed and rejected the six teacher demands and explained the arguments for the rejection. He then presented the teachers' negotiation team with four counterproposals:

1. A $300-per-year increase for all increments in the salary schedule would be effective September, 1967.
2. Principals would allow teachers more latitude in the content and method of teaching, but textbook selection would remain a discretion of the principals.
3. One teacher aide would be hired for each of the twelve elementary schools to assist in non-teaching duties and clerical operations.
4. Teachers would report for duty one week before school opened to participate in teacher-training programs.

The Twelfth Session: Negotiations End

For several days, the offering and rejection of proposals and counterproposals continued. Finally, the non-economic demands were settled; after five more days of negotiating, the parties came to terms on the economic issues. The results of the first contract negotiation in the Glenco school system were as follows:

1. The base salary for beginning teachers with no experience would be increased by $350 per year, and each succeeding increment in the present salary schedule would be increased by $300. Salary increases would be effective September 1, 1967.
2. Two teacher aides would be hired for each elementary school and one for each of the junior and senior high schools for purposes of relieving teachers of non-teaching and clerical duties.
3. Effective September, 1967, maximum classroom size for one teacher would be thirty students. For any class in excess of thirty students, the teacher would be assisted by another full- or part-time teacher or a teacher aide.
4. A personal leave allowance would be made for teachers with two years of full-time experience in the Glenco school system to take effect according to the following schedule:
    a) teachers with two to six years experience at Glenco, one personal leave day per year;
    b) teachers with six or more years experience at Glenco, two personal leave days per year.
5. Teachers would report to school one week before school was

scheduled to open to participate in pre-school workshops aimed at the improvement of instruction. A combined teacher-administrator committee would be responsible for planning and conducting the workshop. Teachers would be paid an additional $150 for this extra week of professional activity.

The school board prepared a formal agreement as requested by the teacher organizations and the latter accepted it in its entirety. Newspaper photographers and reporters were called in to take pictures of the two teams of negotiators; the president of the school board sat with the negotiators for these pictures. A joint release was issued to the press reporting the successful proceedings, including the pre-school workshop program.

The ratification by the school board and two teacher organizations of the first agreement was indeed a major step for the teachers of the Glenco School District. Although the school board had not conceded all of the issues originally proposed, the teachers for the first time in the school's history had their terms of employment in written form, a basis from which future sources of discontent could be eliminated.

The Grievance Procedure

Prior to the ratification of the agreement, the school board's negotiation team and the teachers' joint-negotiation committee devised a semi-formal grievance procedure to be incorporated in the written contract. It was established that any complaint about a violation of the agreement should be settled in the lowest possible of the four following steps:

Steps	Representative of Teacher Organization	Representative of Employer	Time Limit
Step 1	School Representative	Principal	4 days
Step 2	Grievance Committee	Superintendent	10 days
Step 3	Grievance Committee and Presidents of NEA and AFT	Board of Education	15 days

Step 4 Arbitration by mutually selected ad hoc arbitrator

The adequacy of the new grievance procedure was not tested until October, 1967. At the start of the fall semester, Alicia Genster, one of Glenco's second-grade teachers, was assigned a class of thirty students. Late in September, a new student was assigned to Mrs. Genster's class, but no objection was made. In October, a second-grade student was transferred out of a special-education class and placed in Mrs. Genster's class, making a class size of thirty-two. Annoyed at being given two new students in mid-semester, especially since she had started with a large class, Mrs. Genster complained to the school grievance representative.

The grievance representative agreed that the situation was in violation of the contract provision which specified a maximum classroom size of thirty students, and within two days he met with the elementary school principal. The representative proposed that either the two students be transferred to another class or an extra full-time teacher aide be provided to assist Mrs. Genster. The principal's reply was that the student could not be transferred since it would involve daily transportation, and that the hiring of extra aides was not within his authority. Thus, the grievance was passed to the grievance committee.

The grievance committee notified the superintendent of the complaint and of their desire to meet for discussion. Within a week, the meeting with the superintendent was held. He maintained the position that the class should remain as it was since it began the semester with the allowed thirty students, since the addition of the two students was irrelevant to the contract language, and since it would disrupt the educational process of two children if they were removed.

Finding the superintendent's rationale unconvincing, the grievance committee decided to meet with the school board to review the situation. The officials of the NEA and AFT sensed that the future strength of the negotiated agreement could depend upon the outcome of this case. A meeting with the school board was scheduled within the required time limit.

The grievance committee with the officials of the NEA and AFT informed the school board that if appropriate corrections were not instituted, it was their intention to take the case before an arbitrator. Fortunately for both parties, a school-board member was a manager of a Glenco industrial firm and was well versed in grievance handling. This school-board member recognized that the situation was contrary to the terms expressed in the contract, and he further knew that any arbitrator would rule against the school board for this reason. Therefore, the board decided to make an adjustment. To resolve the situation, a teacher aide would be hired to assist Mrs. Genster for the remainder of the first semester. At the beginning of the second semester, two students would be transferred to other classrooms.

In Retrospect

The sources of the discontent in the Glenco school system were not eliminated by the new organization, nor was the educational system itself vastly improved. However, the teachers no longer must resign themselves to the fact that there is little way of producing improvement in their employment conditions and the type of education being provided the community's children. The mere thought that organized effort could bring about eventual change provided a stimulus to the Glenco teachers that improved their morale. However, the school board, teachers, and administrators knew that a great deal more had to be done and that next year's negotiation sessions might prove to be more difficult ones.

7

Services and References

The purpose of this chapter is to acquaint the reader with services and references that are useful to the people involved in collective negotiations, particularly in education.

There are innumerable bibliographies available from various organizations and institutions. The annotated lists presented here are selective, limited, and generally directed toward educators.

SERVICES

1. Educators Negotiating Service, 1507 M Street, N.W., Washington, D.C. 20005.

    This service is a division of Educational Service Bureau, Inc. The Editorial Advisory Board of the service can be classified as "neutral" since it includes representatives from universities, school systems (administrators), and teachers' organizations (AFT and NEA). The service publishes a twice-monthly report plus special reports. Individual service is also available.

2. American Federation of Teachers, 1012 14th St., N.W., Washington, D.C. 20005.

The AFT provides lists of the organization publications dealing with collective bargaining. Included in the lists are such titles as:
"Collective Bargaining and Public Employees"
"Compulsory Arbitration"
"How Collective Bargaining Works"

3. Negotiation Research Digest, Records Division, National Education Association, 1201 16th St., N.W., Washington, D.C. 20036.

The Negotiation Research Digest was first published in 1967. This periodical, prepared by the Research Division of the NEA, contains from forty to fifty pages per issue and has ten issues per year. The digest contains descriptions and analyses, data and statistics, judicial information, negotions agreements, and special items.

4. Negotiations Game, Charles E. Merrill Publishing Co., 1300 Alum Creek Drive, Columbus, Ohio 43216.

The Negotiations Game for Educators was developed through the University Council for Educational Administration and was published by Merrill in January, 1968. The purpose of this real-life simulation is to provide practice for teachers, administrators, and school-board members in collective negotiations. This service publication contains five sections:
  Instructor's Manual
  Short Form (7 negotiating issues)
  Intermediate Form (11 negotiating issues)
  Long Form (20 negotiating issues)
  Evaluation
The negotiating game can be used by local organizations in developing negotiating techniques.

5. Other specific sources of service or information:
   a) American Association of School Administrators, 1201 16th St., N.W., Washington, D.C. 20036.

b) National School Boards Association, 1940 Sheridan Road, Evanston, Ill. 60201.

c) U.S. Office of Education, 400 Maryland Ave., S.W., Washington, D.C. 20202.

d) American Arbitration Association, 140 West 51st St., New York, N.Y. 10020.

e) Federal Mediation and Conciliation Service, Department of Labor Building, Washington, D.C. 20427.

f) National Labor Relations Board, 1717 Pennsylvania Avenue, N.W., Washington, D.C. 20570.

6. Other general sources of service and information:
   a) Local Teachers Organizations;
   b) State Teachers Organizations;
   c) State Associations of School Administrators;
   d) State Associations of School Boards;
   e) State Departments of Education;
   f) State Departments of Labor;
   g) University Departments of Education and Labor Relations.

REFERENCES

ALLEN, ROY B. and JOHN SCHMID, eds., *Collective Negotiations and Educational Administration.* Columbus, Ohio: University Council for Educational Administration, 1965, 126 pp.

This book was published following a U.C.E.A. seminar held at the University of Arkansas. The seminar was directed toward professors of educational administration. There are eight major papers presented in this book. School superintendents should find the book useful.

BRINKMEIER, ORIA A., GERALD C. UBBEN, and RICHARD C. WILLIAMS, *Inside the Organization Teacher.* Danville, Ill.: The Interstate Printers and Publishers, Inc., 1967, 119 pp.

This monograph reports a comprehensive study of the differences between members of a "Professional Association" and a "Teacher Union." Three specific factors are included:
1. teacher knowledge of educational issues;
2. teacher personality characteristics;

3. teacher views on the school environment in which they are employed.

The major focus is on teachers as members of a teacher organization. This monograph should be useful to teachers, administrators, and school-board members.

ELAM, STANLEY M., MYRON LIEBERMAN, and MICHAEL H. MOSKOW, *Readings on Collective Negotiations in Public Education*. Chicago: Rand McNally & Company, 1947, 470 pp.

The three people responsible for this publication served as authors and editors. The book brings together forty-one articles from a variety of sources and covers a wide range of subjects related to collective negotiations. Major headings for this collection of readings are:
- The Background of Collective Negotiations in Public Negotiations;
- The Legal and Political Framework for Collective Negotiations;
- Organizational Approaches to Collective Negotiations;
- Organizational Issues in Collective Negotiations;
- Collective Negotiations and School Administration;
- Strategy and Tactics in Collective Negotiations;
- Special Issues in Collective Negotiations.

This book of readings can be used by anyone interested in broadening his understanding of collective negotiations in public education.

LAW, KENNETH L., *et al.*, *The Manual for Teacher Negotiations*. Windsor, Conn.: Educators' Press, Educational Consultative Services, Inc., 1966, 56 pp.

This paperback manual presents the basic, essential know-hows that teacher groups and their representatives need when they face representatives of school boards across the negotiating table. It contains four major topics:
1. preparation and organization;
2. developing a proposal;
3. techniques of negotiation;
4. resolving a disagreement.

This manual is particularly designed for teachers.

LIEBERMAN, MYRON and MICHAEL H. MOSKOW, *Collective Negotiations for Teachers: An Approach to School Administration*. Chicago: Rand McNally & Company, 1966, 745 pp.

This extensive work is one of the first definitive publications dealing with collective negotiations in education. If one were forced to choose only one reference for study in this field, the Lieberman-Moskow book should rank as one of the top choices. The book contains both background material and information current in 1965-66. The appendices contain large amounts of illustrative material.

LUTZ, FRANK W., LOU KLEINMAN, and SY EVANS, *Grievances and Their Resolution.* Danville, Ill.: Interstate Printers and Publishers, Inc., 1967, 108 pp.

This book is a presentation of a conference on the teacher-administrator-school board relationship held at New York University. The approach of the authors is to describe and analyze the behaviors from which grievances emerge. These behaviors are placed within the context of the school and examined with regard to their relationship to policies and procedure, the application of rules and regulations, and the authority structure of a school organization. The book can be used by local organizations in developing orderly means of resolving differences.

STINNETT, TIMOTHY M., JACK H. KLEINMAN, and MARTHA L. WARE, *Professional Negotiations in Public Education.* New York: The Macmillan Company, 1966, 309 pp.

This book, by three National Education Association writers, presents the case for professional negotiations from the viewpoint of the NEA. The publication is particularly useful for teachers but could be studied to advantage by administrators and board members as well.

MOSKOW, MICHAEL H., *Teachers and Unions.* Philadelphia, Pa.: University of Pennsylvania Press, 1966, 288 pp.

This book was published through the Wharton School of Finance and Commerce, Industrial Research Unit, University of Pennsylvania, following the completion of the author's doctoral dissertation. Dr. Moskow finds no significant difference between the approaches of the AFT and the NEA in regard to the process of collective negotiations. This volume can be very useful to anyone involved in collective negotiations in education.

DOHERTY, ROBERT E. and WALTER E. OBERER, *Teachers, School Boards and Collective Bargaining: A Changing of the*

Guard. Ithaca, N.Y.: New York State School of Industrial and Labor Relations, Cornell University, May, 1967, 139 pp.

This paperback deals with the development of the public school teacher from colonial times to the present. The major emphasis, however, is on the various aspects of legal questions and the manners in which several state statutes deal with these issues. The book is part of a new series initiated by the ILR School at Cornell. The authors are both labor-relations experts: Mr. Doherty has a background in the education area and Mr. Oberer is an attorney specializing in labor law in the public sector. This is an excellent book on legal posture in collective negotiations.

METZLER, JOHN, *A Journal of Collective Negotiations*. Trenton, N.J.: New Jersey State Federation District Boards of Education, 1967, 121 pp.

This paperback is intended as an aid to boards of education, but it can be useful to both sides in the negotiation process. It covers the historical development of the bargaining process, preparation for negotiation, the first agreement, third-party intervention, and evaluating the human element. It includes one negotiation agreement in the appendix.

Index

AAA (*see* American Arbitration Association)
AASA (*see* American Association of School Administrators)
Administrative staff's role, 66-67
Advisory arbitration, 49, 77
AFL-CIO (*see* American Federation of Labor and Congress of Industrial Organizations)
AFT (*see* American Federation of Teachers)
Agreement:
  administration of, 44-46
  written, 43, 55, 70, 72
Allen, Roy B., 105
American Arbitration Association, 18, 49, 74, 79, 81, 105
American Association of School Administrators, 64, 73, 104
American Federation of Labor and Congress of Industrial Organizations, 49, 60
American Federation of Teachers:
  collective bargaining, 59
  defined, 49, 60-61
  exclusive recognition, 17, 73
  growth, 6
  need for, 4
  negotiations:
    approach, 30
    goal, 70
    guidelines, 81
    scope, 21
  philosophy, 60
  reasons for joining, 61
  services, 104
  strikes, 1-2
  superintendent's role, 65
  unit criteria, 16
Arbitration, 49, 77
Arbitrator, 49

Attorneys' role, 34
Authority of school boards, 62
Award, 49

Bakke, E. Wright, 6
Bargaining, defined, 50
Bargain in good faith, 69
Bargaining unit, 14
Behavioral Science and Educational Administration, 4
Behavioral theory, 4
Benson, Charles S., 6
Berlo, David K., 48
Binding arbitration, 77
Board members' role, 34
Board of Education, 50
Board of Trustees, 50
Brinkmeier, Oria A., 105
Budgets, 69
Bureaucratization, 2-3

California, 11, 12-13, 17, 21, 42
Caucus technique, 69
Chamberlain, Neil W., 27, 28
Changing Employment Relationship in Public Schools, The, 7
Checkoff, defined, 50
Civil rights, 58
Closed meetings, 68
Collective bargaining, defined, 50, 59
Collective Bargaining, 27
"Collective Bargaining and Public Employees," 104
Collective negotiations (*see* Negotiations, collective)
Collective Negotiations and Educational Administration, 105
Collective Negotiations for Teachers: An Approach to School Administration, 18, 106
Communications, 47
Company union, 50
Compulsory arbitration, 49
"Compulsory Arbitration," 104
Conciliation, defined, 50
Conciliator, defined, 50
Conflicts of interest, 68, 70
Connecticut, 11, 12-13, 20
Constitution, 10, 60
Contemporary Collective Bargaining, 25
Contract, 51

Index

Contract bar, 19
Cooperative approach, 28

Davey, Harold W., 25, 31
Demands, 51
Doherty, Robert E., 4, 19, 22, 107
Drafting a Union Contract, 44
Dual representation, 75
Dues:
   check-off procedure, 82
   defined, 51

Economic arrangement, 27-28
Economic injustice, 58
"Economic Problem of Education Associated with Collective Negotiation," 6
Educational Service Bureau, Inc., 103
Education revolution, 2
Educators Negotiating Service, 103
Elam, Stanley, 106
Election bar, 19
Employees' rights, 9
Employer-Employee Relationships in the Public School, 6
Ethics, professional, 78
Evans, Sy, 107
Exclusive representation, 16, 51

Fact-finding, 51, 76
Facts for collective negotiations, 80-81
Federal Mediation and Conciliation Service, 79, 105
Fringe benefits, 51

Glass, Ronald W., 1
Good faith, 52
Grievances, 52
Grievances and Their Resolution, 107
Grievance procedure, 76, 79, 80
Griffith, Daniel, 4
Guidelines for negotiation, 35-38
Guidelines for Professional Negotiations in Iowa, 33

Hours, 52
"How Collective Bargaining Works," 104
Human Relations School, 5

Identity, loss of, 58
Impasse, 52, 76
Independent union, 52
Inside the Organization Teacher, 105
Iowa State Education Association, 32
Issue, defined, 52
Items to negotiate, 43

Journal of Collective Negotiations, A, 23, 108
Joint representation, 75

Kleinman, Jack H., 107
Kleinman, Lou, 107
Kuhn, James W., 27, 28

Law, 5
Law, Kenneth L., 106
Language, 49
Language and Communications, 48
Legal right, 60
Legislation, 81-82
Lieberman, Myron, 18, 27, 106
Loss of identity, 58
Lutz, Frank W., 107

Management, defined, 52
Management approach, 28
Management rights, 20
Managerial prerogative, 53
Manual for Teacher Negotiations, The, 106
Marceau, LeRoy 43-44
Market arrangement, 27-28
Massachusetts, 20
Mayo, Elton, 5
Mediation, 53, 76
Mediator, 53, 77
Metzler, John, 23, 108
Michigan, 19
Michigan Labor Mediation Board, 15
Minnesota, 11, 12-13, 16, 22
Minority groups, 76
Miller, George A., 48
Monthly Labor Review, 1
Moskow, Michael H., 18, 27, 106, 107
Mutual respect, 35

Index 113

National Education Association:
  defined, 53, 61
  exclusive recognition, 17, 73
  need for, 4
  negotiations:
    approach, 30, 32
    goal, 70
    guidelines, 81
    professional, 59
    scope, 21
  philosophy, 60
  reasons for joining, 62
  services, 104
  strikes, 1-2
  superintendent's role, 64-65
  unit criteria, 16

National Labor Relations Act, 19
National Labor Relations Board, 105
National School Boards Association, 65, 73, 105
National Society for Study of Education, 4
NEA (*see* National Education Association)
Nebraska, 11, 12-13
Negotiable items, 70, 71
Negotiating committee, 33
Negotiating panel, 63
Negotiating sessions, 68
Negotiation Research Digest, 22, 104
Negotiations:
  administrator's relationship, 40-42
  bilateral, 22, 26
  collective, 25-26, 50, 58, 59
  community relationship, 42
  defined, 53
  election of committee, 39
  framework, 27
  game, 104
  inevitable, 59-60
  multilateral, 26
  preparation, 30-33, 39
  procedure, 34-38
  professional, 53, 59
  progress reports, 39
  reasons, 59
  ritual, 28-29

scope, 20-22
teachers' relationship, 38-40
unilateral, 22, 26
Negotiators, 63, 64
New Jersey, 20, 22
New York, 17
New York City, 29
New York State Public Employee Relations Board, 81
Non-binding arbitration, 77
Non-negotiable items, 71
NSBA (*see* National School Boards Association)
NSSE (*see* National Society for Study of Education)

Oberer, Walter, E., 4, 19, 22, 107
Oregon, 11, 12-13
Organization, defined, 53

Philadelphia, 18
Principal:
  defined, 53
  role, 67
Problem-oriented negotiation, 36
Problem-solving arrangement, 27-28
Process of Communication, The, 48
Professional arrangement, 27-28
Professional ethics, 78
Professionalism, 62, 71
Professional negotiations, 53, 59
Professional Negotiations in Public Education, 107
Proportional representation, 16, 75
Public bargaining, 6
Public employees, 58
Public employment, 5-6

Readings on Collective Negotiations in Public Education, 106
Recognition, 14
  methods, 17
  rights, 72-76
Regulating agency, 81
Representation, 75
Representative, defined, 54
Representative elections, 76
Revolution, education, 2
Rhode Island, 11, 12-13, 20

Salaries, 55, 58, 70
Sanctions, 54, 78
Schmid, John, 105
School board, local, 10
School committee, 50
Settlement, defined, 54
Society, impact of, 5
Sovereignty doctrine, 10-11
Steward, defined, 54
Stinnett, Timothy M., 107
Strike, defined, 54, 78
Strikes and stoppages, 1
Structural relationships, 9
Superintendent, defined, 54
Superintendents' role, 64-67
Supervisor, defined, 54

Taylor, F. W., 5
Teachers, School Boards, and Collective Bargaining: A Changing of the Guard, 4, 107-108
"Teachers, School Boards and Employment Relations," 6
Teachers and Unions, 107
Teacher:
  aggressiveness, 57
  defined, 54
  of today, 3
  professional role, 57
  rights, 10

Ubben, Gerald C., 105
Unit, 55
University Council for Educational Administration, 104
U.S. Office of Education, 105

Voluntary arbitration, 49

Wages, 55
Wagner Act of 1935, 21
Wall Street Journal, 2
Ware, Martha L., 107
Washington, 11, 12-13
Williams, Richard C., 105
Working conditions, 55, 71
Written agreement, 43, 55, 70, 72
"Work Stoppage and Teachers: History and Prospect," 1